Global Justice

Global Justice

An Introduction

Thom Brooks
Durham University
Durham, UK

WILEY Blackwell

Registered Offices
John Wiley & Sons, Inc., 111 River Street, Hoboken, NJ 07030, USA
John Wiley & Sons Ltd, The Atrium, Southern Gate, Chichester, West Sussex, PO19 8SQ, UK

For details of our global editorial offices, customer services, and more information about Wiley products visit us at www.wiley.com.

Library of Congress Cataloging-in-Publication Data Applied for:
Paperback ISBN: 9781405184427

Cover Design: Wiley
Cover Images: © jimmyjamesbond/Getty Images

Set in 10.5/13pt Ehrhardt by Straive, Pondicherry, India
Printed and bound by CPI Group (UK) Ltd, Croydon, CR0 4YY

C9781405184427_160623

For my students

Contents

Preface

When I was an undergraduate student in the 1990s, I developed a lifelong interest in political philosophy. The field has changed in so many ways since. One important way is the shift from a near exclusive look at domestic justice to mainstreaming global justice. With only a handful of exceptions, virtually all talk about justice was really about justice within a state. What was striking at the time is how rarely global justice came up – even though groundbreaking work was ever-present.

Global justice is not new and political philosophers have grappled with it since day one. What is new is the size and scale of interest in the subject over the past few decades. We have always talked about human rights crossing borders, just war theories, climate justice, and much more. But instead of these being fringe topics at the margins of political philosophy, they have moved onto the center stage.

The origins behind this book lie in an earlier book. Nearly two decades ago, there was relatively little in this area for students. I saw a need for a new anthology bringing together the best classic and contemporary work, of readings being widely taught and yet nowhere collected in one place. Blackwell kindly agreed to publish my *The Global Justice Reader* in 2008, and I have been thrilled to see the positive reception it has enjoyed since. This was part of a four-book deal to produce *The Global Justice Reader*, an edited book *Hegel's Philosophy of Right*, a monograph on political philosophy for the Fundamentals in Philosophy series (set to be completed shortly), and a companion introduction – the book in your hands – to

The Global Justice Reader. I am more than a little embarrassed by the length of time in bringing all four books to fruition, as life intervened in several ways including my continuing work in Parliament advising on mostly home affairs and justice issues for over a decade. But I am pleased to have at least produced an extra book – a new revised edition of the original *Reader* expanded, revised, and updated – which I hope has kept me in Blackwell's good books notwithstanding the delays.

As I make clear in the following Introduction, this book can be read and understood as a standalone introduction to global justice or as a companion to either the first or revised edition of *The Global Justice Reader*. It is a great pleasure to see this book appear alongside the revised edition of the *Reader*, and I very much hope students will continue to benefit from both for many more years to come.

My first thanks must go to my students. The original reason for putting the *Reader* together with this companion book was to benefit students first and foremost. I owe thanks to those who took my classes on global justice at both Newcastle and Durham universities. Their insights and probing questions in lectures and seminars as we worked through each of the main readings surveyed here has been as illuminating as it is enjoyable.

My next thanks must go to the team at Blackwell, especially the late Nick Bellorini. His multi-book deal offer was one of my biggest first breaks as a budding academic. I still recall our conversation at a café around the corner from St. Edmund Hall, Oxford, where these plans were agreed. Nick's support for me at that time was incredibly important, and I will always owe him a huge debt of gratitude and miss speaking with him. I am also hugely thankful to Charlie Hamlyn not least for his superb patience as I have brought several projects to completion (and at last).

Various papers, comments, and more have been presented or discussed at a number of universities and institutions, including the Carlsberg Akademi, Edinburgh Fringe, Glasgow Skeptics, International Centre for Parliamentary Studies, Juris North, Public Policy Exchange, the UK Parliament's All-Parliamentary Group on Refugees, and the universities of Arizona State, Baltimore, Boston, City University of New York Graduate School, Edinburgh, Georgia State, Ghent, Hull, Indian Institute of Technology, Jagran Lakecity, Leicester, Oslo, St. Andrews, Stirling, Suffolk, Surrey, University College London, and Yale. I owe many thanks to several friends and colleagues for various conversations helping to shape my views, including Robin Attfield, Christian Barry, Lord (David) Blunkett, David Boucher, Gillian Brock, Claire Brooks, Gary Browning, Vittorio Bufacchi, Carolyn Cole Candolera, Simon Caney, Andrew I. Cohen, Andrew Jason Cohen, James Connolly, Rowan Cruft, Fabian Freyenhagen, Christel Fricke, Lisa

Fuller, Stephen Gardiner, the late John Gardner, Carol Gould, Les Green, Gina Gustavsson, Bruce Haddock, Iain Hampsher-Monk, Nicole Hassoun, David Held, Clare Heyward, Peter Hulm, Afzal Khan MP, Eva Kittay, Alison Jaggar, Peter Jones, Pauline Kleingeld, Melissa Lane, S. Matthew Liao, Kasper Lippert-Rasmussen, Loren Lomasky, Graham Long, the late Jonathan (E.J.) Lowe, Holly Lynch MP, Ruth Macklin, Jeff McMahan, Raino Malnes, Sandra Marshall, Wayne Martin, David Miller, Margaret Moore, Richard Mullender, Aletta Norval, Martin O'Neill, late Gerhard Øverland, Eric Posner, Jon Quong, Peri Roberts, David Rodin, Michael Rosen, Dominic Roser, Lord (Richard) Rosser, Andrea Sangiovanni, Samuel Scheffler, David Schlosberg, Thomas Schramme, Esther Schubert, Peter Singer, Baroness (Angela) Smith, Matthew Noah Smith, Suzanne Sreedhar, Daniel Star, Keir Starmer KC MP, Kok-Chor Tan, Fernando Teson, Laura Valentini, Martin van Hees, Albert Weale, Kit Wellman, Jo Wolff, Hiro Yamazaki, and Lea Ypi among others.

I owe a large debt to Martha Nussbaum, whose work has had a deep impact on me; to Leif Wenar, who first introduced me to the topic; and to Lord (Bhikhu) Parekh, who has been my guru for nearly 20 years. I am enormously grateful to my family, especially to Claire and Eve, for their patience and support throughout the writing of this book and much else.

T.A.K.B.   *Sedgefield, England*

Introduction

Justice for the globe

Malaika does not live like other teenagers in Western countries. Since the civil war began in her country that tragically saw her father killed, before famine or debts took what was left of her family's farm, she struggles to earn what money she has left to help feed her unwell mother and younger siblings. They live each day hand to mouth. With these daunting daily struggles to survive, Malaika is unable to attend school and prepare for a future career.

Joseph lives in a home that his family has owned proudly for several generations. But it will sadly not be around much longer to be enjoyed by his children nor any grandchildren. Joseph's problem is not money or a desire to move away but the rising sea level that now reaches his front gate at each high tide. Joseph's island is sinking and his nation is being slowly drowned. He and his family do not know where else they might go. They have never been abroad before and yet face permanent expulsion as nature swallows up their country.

Emma's life is a world away from Malaika and Joseph. Emma lives in a comfortable home in an affluent and desirable town. She was active in sport, winning a scholarship at university and enjoys a well-paid professional job. Emma is able to afford a home in the best part of town where her children thrive. The family enjoys vacations abroad every summer.

These short biographical snapshots are fictional. None actually exist. However, their circumstances – and their contrasts – are all too real. Malaika, Joseph, and Emma did not choose to be born or where they would grow up. Yet, their future horizons can be shaped by the contexts they find themselves. Growing up in a war-torn famished developing country is different from living on the frontline combatting climate change or enjoying life in an affluent state. But what to do about these differences? If in the same state, we might argue they should have the same life chances and greater equality – but they do not. So, what should justice look like for Malaika, Joseph, and Emma when they have different lives and are citizens of different countries? If you are interested in these issues, then you are interested in *global justice*. Topics like severe poverty, just war, gender global justice, climate change, distributive justice, and much more are all covered in this book.

What is global justice?

Traditionally, whenever political philosophers thought about justice, they primarily focused on justice within a state. Questions about what freedom, equality, and rights individuals might possess were aimed at citizens of a state. For example, John Rawls's famous *A Theory of Justice* (1971) develops a conception of justice that individuals enter at birth and leave at death. Rawls considers what principles of justice that citizens would agree – and how they would do it. Justice is about setting the boundaries and agreeing how we might regulate our society.

But, of course, this raises big questions about what justice looks like more broadly. Should all states around the globe have the same view about justice – or can there be differences? How might "we" resolve conflicts between states that disagree about fundamental issues of justice without a world government or court?[1] Are there rights that everyone is entitled to, even if my state does not recognize them? These are all the big questions that global justice theories attempt to answer – and which will be discussed in this book.

---

[1] A note about the use of "we" at the start. While I write from the perspective of a dual American and British citizen, I do not intend the "we" used here to have any particular characteristics beyond "individuals interested in global justice." We, those who have interests in global justice as a topic, ask these questions wherever we are from.

Global justice is about justice across borders (Brooks 2012; Brooks 2016a). These issues are some of the most pressing and important as well (see Brooks 2015a). Our world is divided. There are some highly affluent states that control most of the global wealth. Yet, there are many states where individuals suffer in severe poverty. So, what should be done? Some might argue that those who can supply the resources to save others in need should do so, but others claim the primary responsibility should be with those responsible for their severe poverty. Which should we choose?

We live in a world of borders. Nobody chooses where they are born. And yet, where we are born can influence our life chances in terms of health, education, and relative wealth. So, what should we do about immigration? Some might argue that our citizenship at birth is arbitrary because we did not choose where we were born. It is unfair to deny individuals an opportunity to live where they wish and so, it is argued, we should have more open borders. However, others argue how a society is structured is not arbitrary. Communities self-determine themselves and invest in their citizens, such as in public services that require border restrictions for such support to be maintained. Which view to support?

We live in an endangered world (Brooks 2020a). Climate change is threatening our future sustainability in a myriad of ways, such as increased risks of flooding coastal communities, worsening famines, and more severe weather events. Some claim we should turn to conservationism cutting back global emissions substantially, even if it cut economic growth, as a means to bring climate change to a stop. Others argue that we should invest in adaptative technologies to adjust better to changing conditions. Which should be our priority?

These are only a few of the many important issues that global justice deals with – and covered here. This book is an introductory guide surveying the main ideas from some of the key texts in the field by its leading contributors.

What is this book about?

This book is divided into 11 chapters. In this section, a brief overview of the topics and issues are surveyed. The aim is to provide a general picture of what different areas of global justice are about. Readers are welcome to organize their approach in which order they consider chapters afterward.

The first chapter is about *sovereignty*. This is about the supreme authority within a territory. This is a core concept in global justice. The idea of sovereignty might imply a supreme *legitimate* authority. Some philosophers, like Thomas Hobbes, argued that sovereignty was built on the consent of the governed. It raises questions about what makes any governing body a legitimate authority – and whether any such body lacking public consent can be considered a supreme authority. Moreover, it also raises questions about whether other states should consider a political community as a sovereign state and why.

The idea of sovereignty, at least in Hobbes's influential work, is connected to his idea of a state of nature. He argues that a world without government where we are each left to fend for ourselves is an environment where life is harsh and short-lived. Hobbes claims we would each crave security in self-preservation and so would come together surrendering our freedom to act as we like in a state of nature to consent to a strong government. Limiting our individual freedom and consenting to having the state regulate our relations is a price worth paying, he argues, for peace.

As will be seen, this idea about how we might legitimize the power of the state for its citizens has been applied to the international sphere. It is regularly argued that there is a global state of nature as individual states fend for themselves without a world government or state to govern their relations. The ensuing debate is whether this analogy of an amoral global sphere is a correct description of foreign affairs or whether there are normative requirements globally as constructed by states in cooperation with each other.

The second chapter is about *rights to self-determination*. This takes discussion about sovereignty a step further. So, what justifies any group of individuals to form a state? What values or principles, if any, must they all accept? Is it necessary that group members recognize each other and, if so, how? And, furthermore, if a group can legitimately form a state, can they do so by seceding from an existing state – and those that state have a say?

The issues are thorny, but fundamental. We often recognize the right of sovereign states to regulate themselves without foreign interference in peacetime. So, what, if any, limits are there to how a state self-determines itself and governs its citizens? And what if citizens are deeply divided on such issues to the extent that agreement on basic governance seems beyond reach? While we might often claim a right to self-determination, it is not always clear how this might work in theory or practice. But it is very clear that – whatever our view – there may be far-reaching consequences for understanding the state and its relation to other states.

The third chapter is about *human rights*. It was once thought that there was a divine right of kings whereby only the monarch had rights – and any rights their subjects enjoyed would be at the pure discretion of a king or queen. Supporters of natural rights objected and claimed that individuals had rights *naturally*, from birth, and regardless of their nationality. This raises a fundamental question of whether rights are ours from birth – and a part of nature – or whether the rights we have come from social conventions over time.

A further fundamental question is, if I have human rights naturally or socially, which rights do I have? This touches on one distinction between our *rights* versus our *human rights*. The latter are usually thought to be more essential and universal. While many argue that rights to life or liberty are human rights, not every right shares the same status. Plus, there are deep disagreements about what should be seen as a human right. For example, most accept a right to life but not everyone agrees a right to life must mean we abolish the death penalty. Thinking about human rights helps us better understand our most fundamental freedoms, what it is that gives them a special status and reflect on disagreements about their status, number, and justification.

The fourth chapter is about *nationalism and patriotism*.[2] In the political science literature, discussions about (classical) nationalism typically refer to right-wing political movements.[3] But here we refer to a kind of *ethical* nationalism referred to as "liberal nationalism." In other words, what features and values should members of a nation possess in common – and how can this be justified? Is national membership a matter of birth or how might citizens from other states join the national community? And, more centrally, are we under a greater obligation to help conationals in need over non-nationals?

Patriotism is often held as a kind of virtue – that it is praiseworthy to be patriotic and supportive of the country of your citizenship. But what are the grounds for such commitment – and what are the limits? Do we have equal

---

[2] Some readers will notice that I did not name John Rawls's *The Law of Peoples* and its critics. This was the fourth section of the original edition of *The Global Justice Reader*. As this appears to be covered much less in global justice courses now, I have decided to remove the section from the revised *Reader*. I have added a new section later in the book on Immigration and Citizenship which is getting greater prominence instead and cover it in Chapter 6.

[3] A brief note that this book will take an interdisciplinary perspective. This is because my background is across disciplines with a BA in music and political science, an MA in political science, an MA in philosophy, a PhD in philosophy, eight years working in Politics department, and another decade in a law school, half of which was spent as dean. I will draw on this background throughout this text. For what it is worth, I strongly recommend academic study across disciplines as a way of enriching multidisciplinary studies generally.

duties to everyone – or special duties to compatriots that prioritize them over others? Does a love of country clash with commitments to love non-citizens or not?

The fifth chapter is about *cosmopolitanism* and continues to engage with questions raised about nationalism and patriotism. For example, are liberal nationalists right that we have special duties to our fellow citizens over others – or are cosmopolitans right that we universal duties toward human beings regardless of their nationality? What does cosmopolitan justice look like in an international sphere of separate states?

A major debate in cosmopolitan thought is about whether world peace requires a world government. Can we aspire to a perpetual peace among states without a single global power ruling over all states – and, if not, why not? There are further issues around the importance of the equality of every individual in a world where life chances can differ wildly depending on where someone is born. What does global justice have to say about this? These are some of the questions we will be looking at more closely in that chapter.

The sixth chapter is about *immigration and citizenship*.[4] People are crossing borders more than ever before. This is a topic that is personal to me. I was born in the United States where I had citizenship and then studied and worked in the Republic of Ireland before settling and gaining a second citizenship in the United Kingdom. The first question here is simply why have borders? We live in a bordered world, but where the lines are drawn – and what the rules for entry and settlement might be – differ. What justifies restrictions and exclusions? And how – and why – might we treat refugees differently from other forms of migration? It is worth noting that we frequently do. While most immigration rules fall under domestic law, the rules relating to handling asylum claims fall under international law. The former relates mostly to economic migrants and family reunion, while the latter cover individuals fleeing persecution. Most states treat migrants differently depending on their reasons for seeking entry and residence – how and why might this matter?

The seventh chapter is about *global poverty*. This is possibly *the* biggest topic of interest in global justice. The issue is what to do about severe poverty? There are different views on what is best. One is that we may have a positive duty to help if we can irrespective of whether we have any connection

---

[4] Some readers will notice that this is a new section introduced into the revised edition of *The Global Justice Reader* published in 2023. Readers using the original 2008 edition can still follow the references given in this chapter.

to those in need. A second view is that those who may have contributed in some way to those in need have a negative duty to provide support. A third view is we should consider the connections each state has in weighing up the strength or its so-called remedial responsibilities – in other words, its responsibilities to provide a remedy. A related but fourth view is that states are not the only agents of global justice and we should consider the ability and connectedness of nongovernmental international institutions who may have more resources and be placed in a better position to do good.

This work focuses on a central problem. Sadly, there are many in dire need. The question is whether it matters why they are in need if there are those among us who can provide rescue. Or whether those who have done wrong or supported institutions contributing to severe poverty should bear a heavier burden than others.

And when thinking about what should be done, how relevant is what *can* be done? This is where ideal global justice theory focusing on what ought to happen comes against nonideal (or more practical) global justice theorizing which takes more seriously the relevance of our practices on what actions we support.

The eighth chapter is about another big topic in global justice: *just war*. There have been theories about what constitutes a just war since wars were first fought. The classic view is that a just war requires that there is a just cause, fought in a just way by a just government. But, of course, each of these is question-begging. What constitutes a just cause for war? Must we wait for the first strike to hit before taking action – or can we move pre-emptively? What are the limits of lethal combat especially where so much depends on the "just" side winning? And who is to decide what constitutes a just government – cannot non-democracies have a just cause, too?

This literature has expanded greatly over the past decade, especially thanks to the work of an old friend, Jeff McMahan. He challenges the conventional view of just war theory whereby combatants on each side facing each other in battle were thought to have moral symmetry. For McMahan and many others since, only combatants with a just cause can fight as they deny the moral symmetry claiming unjust combatants have no justified right to fight back. But if we think anyone who contributes to an unjust cause might be liable to attack, does this extend to noncombatants in any circumstances? And if we think the distinction of unjust versus just combatant builds of a particular understanding of self-defense between individuals – is this based on a mistake about how self-defense works in the criminal law?

The ninth chapter is about *terrorism*. Famously, former US President Ronald Reagan once said that one man's terrorist is another man's freedom fighter. For example, leaders of the American Revolution are held up as heroes in my native United States. However, this is not true for the leaders of other revolutionary activities using violence. So, how might, if at all, acts of terrorism ever be justified in theory or in practice? What must be intended – and how, if at all, does this matter?

The tenth chapter is about *women and global justice*. Women voices feature in the earlier chapters – and this is important because women philosophers make some of the most profound contributions to the subject.[5] In this chapter, we focus specifically on women and global justice. For example, many of us will agree that our state should do more to champion the rights of women. At the same time, many will agree we should go further in defending multicultural rights. But, is multiculturalism bad for women, especially where some of the practices may appear to undermine the equality between men and women? And how does a feminist view of global justice shape our approach to severe poverty alleviation? Is polygamy acceptable where virtually all polygamous marriages are of one husband with multiple wives – or not?

The final eleventh chapter is about *climate change*. Our planet is warming and human beings are primarily responsible for it. The question is then what to do. One approach is to argue we must focus on conservationism and so substantially reduce our carbon emissions to a sustainable level. A second approach is to claim we should look to technology and find new ways to adapt to our climate changed future. Noticeably, both approaches share a view that there is a happy ever after end-state in sight. If only we conserved or adapted enough, we can continue on – the problem of climate change can be solved. But there is another view that such a position is based on a mistake given that environmental catastrophes have happened without human causes in the past and so suggest that even if we reduced impact to zero or adapted perfectly that this might never be enough to avoid a future catastrophe. And so we should not look at sustainability as a permanent state but as an impermanent state. This raises all kinds of questions. How much should we conserve – and what if no amount of conservation could avoid a catastrophe? Climate change is already happening and so how can we better adapt to it? And how does an ever-present possibility of a future catastrophe impact the way we should think about climate change ethics and the motivation to act?

---

[5]This is an important point. In thinking about the diversity of voices in this subject, these voices should never be collected and restricted in chapters away from the central, mainstream issues. Moreover, this debate discussed here between multiculturalism and feminism is among the most referenced in the field.

In describing these 11 chapters, readers will note that rather than dropping big names I have raised philosophical questions. It is through questions like this that help us think about what a topic is and begin working out for ourselves what our own view might be on these issues. Give yourself time to pause and think – even briefly – about where your intuitions are on these questions and let yourself be challenged by the deeper discussions in the following chapters. We can all think philosophically even if we have not been trained to do so before. This book will support how you might do it, and each chapter ends with discussion questions to reflect on afterward.

How to read this book

This book *Global Justice: An Introduction* is written to be read in two ways. First, it is a standalone text in its own right for students coming to the study of global justice for the first time. No previous knowledge of the topic is assumed nor of philosophy generally in – what I hope – is an accessible and enjoyable survey of the field.

Second, this *Introduction* can be read as a companion to my *The Global Justice Reader*.[6] Each chapter in the *Introduction* covers a section of readings in the *Reader*. For example, Chapters 1 and 2 in the *Introduction* cover the material reprinted in parts 1 and 2 of the *Reader*. To keep the connections simple, I have named each chapter and parts the same so easily connected together. I have kept references to a minimum and mostly to the chapters in the *Reader*, but note where chapter sections discuss different sections in the *Reader* in the footnotes.

This *Introduction* was written from Introduction to Conclusion, and some references may look forward to future chapters, but the chapters may be read in any order of interest and designed to engage and explain students who have not looked at this material previously – although it is hoped this book will be of interest to students who have familiarity, too. Each chapter ends with discussion questions to be thought about individually or in conversation if used as part of a course.

Otherwise, my hope is that students will be introduced to many of the core concepts, debates, and leading contributors. No such book can cover everything, and I have been selective, especially focusing primarily on following the content in the *Reader* and the points raised in the main literature

---

[6] See Brooks (2008, 2023a). This book – *Global Justice: An Introduction* – comments on all chapters from *both* editions and so the Introduction is a companion to either edition albeit more closely following the current 2023 edition.

included in that book. While this Introduction is designed as a helpful survey, readers are always encouraged to explore the primary works cited and discussed to consider their arguments firsthand and develop their own views on various topics.

Global justice is a fascinating subject where interest continues to grow. I hope this book helps make clear why this is.

1

Sovereignty

Introduction

Sovereignty is a central concept in global justice. It concerns the exercise of legitimate power over others, including the limits of its exercise and the forms it might take. In short, sovereignty is about the supreme political authority within a territory (Philpott 2020).

This concept has two important parts. The first is that sovereignty is about *supreme* authority, not *any* lesser form of authority. For example, in medieval England, there were varieties of overlapping authorities that might be appealed to, including the law of the local king, the Danelaw of the Vikings, or canon law (Rabin 2020; Stenton 1971). If accused of breaking the law, the defendant could – and often did – challenge which law (and its associated punishment) should have standing in that case. Trials were not only about who did what, but also about which rules applied. This is an illustration of multiple, overlapping authorities competing for supremacy in the absence of overarching sovereignty.[1] Sovereignty is achieved when

---

[1] Few, if any, introductions to political theory note the multiple, overlapping legal authorities in place during this time. Readers interested in learning more should consult Rabin (2020) and Stenton (1971), as well as Jenkins (1986) which translates the law of Hywel Dda (or "Hywel the Good" translated from the Welsh) which united most of Wales in 942 after a period where Wales was made up of different countries.

Global Justice: An Introduction, First Edition. Thom Brooks.
© 2023 John Wiley & Sons Ltd. Published 2023 by John Wiley & Sons Ltd.

there is a source of political and legal power that has supremacy – and which happened in England over time as power was consolidated and took control.

The second part to sovereignty is it is within a territory.[2] The exercise of supreme political authority has boundaries and sits within a geographical space. Sovereignty is concerned with the supreme authority within a place and that is grounded. Therefore, it might be that a country might not have sovereignty over the full span of its territory if it does not have supreme authority over all space within its borders.

The idea that a supreme authority within a territory establishes sovereignty is influential. Since at least the Peace of Westphalia in 1648, states were deemed to be self-contained, independent, and sovereign bodies in international affairs – in what has been called the state-centric *Westphalian system*. Diplomacy was about respecting the sovereignty of states and their territorial integrity. This meant that any internal matters within a state's territory were seen as a matter for that state alone to act on. No state ought to interfere in the domestic affairs of any other sovereign state.

In this chapter, we will consider two important perspectives on sovereignty and its importance. The first is a classic view drawn from the history of political thought championed by Thomas Hobbes. The second is a contemporary view made prominent by Charles Beitz. Together, they help deepen our understanding of this important political concept and key terminology that will be useful when thinking about other areas of global justice, too.

The state of nature

So, how does sovereignty arise and what justifies it? The classic view stems from philosopher Thomas Hobbes in his work *Leviathan* published in 1651. Hobbes considers the issue of how the state is justified. He reflects on what the world would be like without any state or political institutions, which he calls a *state of nature*.

Individuals in a state of nature live without any rules imposed on them by others. Hobbes says that we are each free to do what we like for the preservation of our own life – the right to life being a fundamental, natural right from birth – in a lawless world governed only by anarchy (Hobbes 1996:86–100).[3] A state of nature is not a happy environment for all. Hobbes describes the state of nature as a condition of war "of every one

---

[2] This is sometimes referred to as "territoriality".

[3] See *The Global Justice Reader*, chapter 1.

against every one" where life is "nasty, brutish and short" (Hobbes 1996:89). As everyone seeks to preserve their own lives, they can come into conflict with others in a world without governance. No one has any safety nor security to protect and preserve themselves. It is not difficult to imagine how difficult such a life could be for even the most able in excellent health.

Hobbes argues that because everyone seeks their own preservation in a world plagued by anarchy and potential conflict we will each seek to obtain peace. Conflict is only considered where peace cannot be secured. Hobbes says it is a "fundamental law of nature" that all individuals seek peace and enjoy it. We do not naturally seek to be at war with one another – not least as this can be counterproductive to each of us seeking our own preservation. We can live longer in greater safety if peace could be secured in some sustainable way. The issue is how this is possible for individuals in this hostile environment.

Hobbes claims that our desire for peace leads us to the second fundamental law of nature (reprinted in the original Old English):

> That man be willing, when others are so too, as farre-forth, as for Peace, and defence of himself he shall think it necessary, to lay down this right to all things; and be contented with so much liberty against other men as he would allow other men against himself. (Hobbes 1996:92)

The argument is as follows. If individuals continued to choose to act with complete freedom doing whatever they wanted whenever they liked, conflict would continue and all of us would remain "in the condition of Warre" (Hobbes 1996:92). The reason is our wants and desires could not always be satisfied at the same time all of the time – especially without rules or guidance that could constrain and direct us.

Peace is made possible when we each choose to *not* exercise our original right to act however we like. Instead, we must all agree "to lay down this right" and "be contented" with less liberty in return for peace. The price of peace is everyone not trying to get their way all the time. But the benefit is everyone is better able to enjoy their freedom and preserve themselves. For Hobbes, the benefits outweigh the costs.

Hobbes speaks throughout about "nature" and what is "natural." This means what is given, such as from birth. For example, a state of nature is how the world was originally – and what could return if peace is ended and we return to our natural condition of being in conflict with one another. Another example is his speaking of a natural right to preserve our lives. This right is natural insofar as it is our right from birth. This view was controversial at Hobbes's time not least as the doctrine of the divine right of kings remained prevalent. This doctrine claimed that any rights we possess was in the gift of our king to bestow upon us – and at the king's discretion (Filmer 1991). In contrast, the natural rights tradition that Hobbes helps establish claims we have individual rights at birth – and independently of any king.[4]

But if we should all surrender some part of our freedom to secure our collective peace and preservation, how does this work? Our natural rights are ours. Hobbes argues that any choice to constrain our freedom must be voluntarily made. We all agree – and consent – together that our freedom should be restricted to secure peace. This voluntary agreement among equal individuals is what Hobbes calls a social "contract" made to further the good to each consenting member (Hobbes 1996:94).

This idea of a social contract plays a major role in political philosophy. It is a means through which it can be argued that governments have legitimacy. Governments are legitimate because they are supported by the consent of the governed. In contrast, governments that do not have the consent of those they govern are not seen as legitimate because there is no social contract in place.

While important, the idea of a social contract is also to some extent mythical. Hobbes argues we do make a social contract and so leave the state of nature, but this "contract" between individuals is not a signed agreement from the past that we see for ourselves. The situation is hypothetical, but Hobbes believes it is realistic. We are not to be persuaded because it is any specific individuals who agree to any particular deal, but because we can each imagine what a state of nature would be like, why we would want to leave it and why our voluntary consent to be governed is what grounds the legitimacy of a political community as a *sovereign body*.

Hobbes claims that we would transfer our freedom to choose individually for ourselves on all matters to another is called *the sovereign* (Hobbes 1996:121–122). This sovereign is the ultimate political authority within our territory and its justification stems from the voluntary consent of all in a social contract. For Hobbes, the head of this state is a monarch to whom we transfer our right to act however we like. Instead of everyone having their way and creating conflicts, what is just is determined by the monarch, to whose rule we have consented. We are punished for breaking the king's laws because we have consented to it, in all agreeing to the sovereign's rule in return for peace and security.

---

[4] It is Hobbes's insistence that we each have individual rights that is behind his being considered a classic liberal.

Perhaps few of us would consent to such an arrangement. Hobbes' position is helpful in many ways regardless of whether we would agree to give up our freedoms like this. His view that anarchy is like a state of nature has been influential and often used to describe international politics. Hobbes's claim that everyone has a natural right to self-preservation of their life is also widely held. While we might not all accept that we must consent a transfer of our liberty to a single monarch to enjoy peace and security, Hobbes believes this will come off the back of reducing conflict. His challenge is that anything less will accept some degree of conflict between individuals, and he invites us to consider how it might be avoided.

Might is not right – nor sovereignty

When thinking about a supreme authority, it might be tempting to say it is the will of the strongest.[5] This is because someone or a group can control a territory through force, such as through its military. It might be said that those who have the ability to control have supreme power – and, so, possess sovereignty. Is this compelling?

This raises a central issue about sovereignty, namely, whether the power it exerts is justified and legitimate or not. For example, take the view that might is right. Justice is determined by whoever wields the biggest stick. Such individuals or groups could be able to force others to obey their rules, but the raw show of strength or threat of violence is not a right to do so.

The idea of might as right is rendered more problematic when we consider other relevant factors. It is common to claim that all individuals have moral equality – and so the state should not give some a greater vote than others, for example. If individuals were treated equally, we could not justify some having power over others because they were able to better coerce others to get their own way.

Hobbes shows us that might is not right. The justification for the state is based on the free and equal consent of citizens. We can extend this idea to how we think about democratic politics.[6] The legitimate authority of a democratic state is through the consent of the governed, expressed

---

[5] Readers interested in history of political thought should see Plato's *The Republic* and Socrates's debate with Thrasymachus, who defends the claim that "justice is nothing other than the advantage of the stronger" (Plato 1992:14 [338]).

[6] It should be noted that Hobbes's idea that all should consent to be ruled did not entail rule by a democratic government, but instead a monarch (see Hobbes 1996).

through free and fair elections.[7] It is through such collective agreement political authority can be justified and a government is legitimized as sovereign, for example. Might is not right, but right can possess might where sovereign power is justified.

International politics as a state of nature

One of the ways in which Hobbes's description of a state of nature *among individuals* has been used is as a description of a situation *among individual states*. In the former, individuals have precarious lives as everyone is free to do anything and so the risk of frequent conflicts is high. The state of nature is a context that we all seek to leave as quickly as possible to embrace the comfort and security of long-lasting peace – by consenting to put ourselves under the authority of another. But things seem different with the latter. Each state is considered a sovereign individual in an anarchic world without order where conflict and war are unavoidable and a part of the realist paradigm about the reality of global affairs. There is no morality at the global level.[8]

This is a view of international anarchy that not all accept. For example, Charles Beitz (1999) considers the possibility of a *normative* international political theory.[9] His target is Hobbes's idea of the state of nature and its potential relevance to understanding global issues. Beitz (1999:13) claims that Hobbes's view represents a kind of international skepticism where moral judgments are thought to have no place. In a state of nature, there is no world government or authority to regulate conflicts. Every state pursues its own interests and seeks its own self-preservation. These interests can collide with others as a matter of fact and there is no higher judge with any authority over states to say which is acting rightly or wrongly. Or so the argument goes.

Beitz challenges the idea – based in Hobbes's account – that a common judge or sovereign – is necessary for states to acknowledge and adhere to moral principles. For Beitz (1999:27), making moral judgments does not

---

[7]The history of political thought has a great many leading figures defending democracy in this way – and, so too, non-democracies. There are debates about what form of government is most justified and not least on what kind of democracy is best – for example, should we support a presidential or parliamentary system? Readers can decide for themselves. The main point here is that democracies are the most popular for justifying political authority among political philosophers.

[8]For the benefit of Hobbes scholars, a more strict view would be to say there is *not much* morality at the global level. Individual natural rights to self-preservation would remain as would the laws of nature.

[9] *The Global Justice Reader*, chapter 2.

require a universal judge. Part of the reason can be found in reconstructing part of Hobbes's arguments. For example, Hobbes claims individuals seek to leave the state of nature for a life regulated by the laws of nature where there are rights and obligations. A state of nature is *politically* anarchic without any political or legal institutions, but it is not *morally* anarchic in that everyone has the same natural rights. The absence of political authority does not entail a lack of moral principles.

Beitz argues that morality exists at the international level. We live in an increasingly interdependent world. All across the globe, states have become increasingly interdependent and cooperate through shared institutions. Various examples include bodies such as the International Monetary Fund and the World Bank. For Beitz, when we look at international politics, it is not a normative-free zone where self-interest is pursued by however a state may wish to do so. States comply with a range of international norms and rules which is evidenced in their working together in international economic bodies and others, like the European Union or NATO. Such institutions would be impossible in a war of one against all – and they can help reduce, if not prevent, conflict to promote peace and security without a need for a world state.

Moreover, as we will explore more in Chapter 8, norms have arisen in terms of the rules of war and diplomacy. For example, there are widely shared international norms governing when military action can be justified and how any such action might be waged with potential consequences for breaches. This is not from the heavens, but as agreed among states across the world. Of course, there are serious questions to raise about how universal these norms might be, how to respond when states disagree about these norms, and how breaches are dealt with – and this will be looked at in more detail in Chapter 8.

But what can be said here is that notwithstanding the influence of Hobbes's idea of a state of nature as a depiction of international politics, we might question – like Beitz does – what this model should tell us. Hobbes claims life in a state of nature will lead us to seek safety and security in a sovereign ruling over us and to who we cede some of our freedom. When applied to global justice, Beitz claims we need not have a world authority to have global norms that enjoy wide support and which matter.

One final point before proceeding. Beitz is talking about Hobbes's state of nature which Hobbes describes as giving rise to a state – as applied to international politics, a sphere of many states. In his work, Beitz is clear that while there is a different lesson to draw from Hobbes's idea that often noted, Beitz recognizes that the analogy goes only so far and that the domestic sphere is different from the international sphere. This is an important qualification we will see arise in other contexts.[10] It suggests that the state-of-nature idea does not mean that states in the international sphere require a higher power, such as a world government, to regulate their activities – without denying that this may not be true of domestic politics. However, it is worth reflecting separately that if peace and security can be secured internationally without a world government having sovereignty of its own, then it may be worth considering alternative power structures for domestic politics – although this is an issue we will not visit here.[11] States pursue their individual interests, but have reasons to cooperate and avoid some of the problems that Hobbes assumes a state of nature would entail.

Global justice and sovereignty

Let us now consider a third view. Thomas Pogge (1992) recommends that we consider sovereignty in a new light.[12] He starts from the position of *individualism* whereby the individual is the ultimate unit of concern. He then considers what he calls *moral cosmopolitanism* understood as the view that "all persons stand in certain moral relations to one another" such that we are required to respect each other's moral status as worthy of equal respect and concern (Pogge 1992:49). The idea is that this creates duties toward others, such as a duty against imposing unjust institutional regimes on distant others. It is because doing so would mean that I did not uphold my duty of treating others as worthy of equal respect and concern, with the assumption that I would not want to live in an unjust institutional regime myself.

Pogge notes that anywhere and everywhere states govern with preeminent authority within a territory. Moreover, these states are also involved in supranational decisions, such as intergovernmental bargaining, with consequences for other states. This is a significant problem as some sovereign polities, like affluent states, bear responsibility for global institutional structures that create and maintain severe poverty in other states. "We," as members of an affluent state, are significant participants in this institutional injustice. Citizens of affluent states have a responsibility to the global poor through the global order our states maintain. Because we are responsible for a serious harm, we have a duty to cease harming and repair the damage.

---

[10] For example, see Chapter 8 on just war theory.
[11] Readers interested in exploring such ideas more might consider Heider and Lewis (1994).
[12] See *The Global Justice Reader*, chapter 3.

However, we might then worry that however compelling the moral justification for this cosmopolitan perspective on harm caused to the global poor through the global institutional order, we uphold that our cosmopolitan solution violates state sovereignty and, therefore, should be abandoned. Alternatively, we might think that, if correct, Pogge's views would lead us to endorse a world state: an effective political body that would have legitimate control over all peoples in order to protect the rights of human beings, defending the person as our ultimate unit of moral concern.

On the contrary, Pogge does not defend a world state largely on the grounds that such a body would be impractical. Instead, he favors a wide distribution of sovereignty among individual (democratic) states, rather than one body. This might be exercised in the following way. Suppose our current state supported global institutions contributing to severe poverty, but this was untrue of a state that was bordering ours. One recommendation is that we should have the option, if the bordering state agreed, to secede from our state and join our neighbor. The sovereignty of a state requires moral support – and where, for Pogge, moral cosmopolitanism is denied we should have the right to be governed by others who accept our responsibilities.

In essence, Pogge (1992:73) speaks of "the right to change" our political status. Sovereignty has been seen as a top–down–like concept about the supreme power over those within its territory. Pogge's example reminds that the legitimacy of sovereignty is not assumed and, following Hobbes, it flows from consent. Where individuals lack consent in support for a sovereign power, it loses its force – and perhaps with the implications that sovereignty might fragment from one sovereign state to several smaller bodies, if we take seriously the equality of individuals.

This points us toward our next chapter's topic of the right to self-determination. But what is of value here is the claim that sovereign power is never a given, nor does it have any right in itself, once established, to permanency. States are regularly challenged and maps redrawn, usually in the direction of new states breaking off from the old. Before turning to how such movements might be justified, it is worth acknowledging this shifting nature of sovereignty, and that its power flows in two directions both from the people and to the people. And, finally, the relation of our state to others can have an effect on both states.

Conclusion

Sovereignty is a key concept of global justice. It is the supreme power within a territory. In this chapter, we have considered both classic and contemporary perspectives on what it is and how it might work. For Hobbes, sovereignty is of the state and is legitimized by individuals wishing to leave the state of nature. That state of nature pushes them on to form a state to regulate their activities as they strive for peace.

Hobbes's idea of a state of nature has been influential, but questions have been raised about whether his conclusions follow from his arguments. For example, many consider the international sphere to be like a state of nature. So, does it require a world government for peace? Hobbes did not support any such body, but also thought war to be inevitable in a sphere where states seek their own advantage amidst a lack of any adjudicating global body.

Beitz disagrees. He claims that peace is possible without a world government. This can be made to manifest through the cooperation of states in transnational institutions. Moreover, through this coordination, global norms have emerged in governing trade and conflict. The state is sovereign, but does not interact alone.

Finally, for Pogge, state sovereignty has limits. No state has the right to impose rights violations on others, such as through coercive institutions that create and maintain severe poverty. We must treat all other individuals with equal concern and respect. When our state fails to do this – including through supporting coercive institutions – we have a right to break away and join with others as new members of a neighboring state, if they agree. The respect of state sovereignty is not merely the task of respecting the sovereignty of other states but of respecting the relationship of states to each other within a global order.

These three different perspectives are intended to show that sovereignty is not one thing. Nor is it thought of in the same way. Readers should ask themselves: what makes a state legitimate? What justifies the state's ability to coerce its citizens? How important is the consent of the government and what should happen when it is gone? It is hoped that readers will have a stronger grasp of some of these issues and be able to consider them more clearly before turning to the right of self-determination in Chapter 2.

Discussion questions

1. What is sovereignty – and is it a useful concept?
2. Was there ever a state of nature and, if so, what would it be like?
3. Why should individuals choose to live in a sovereign state instead of a state of nature?
4. Why and how should states respect the sovereignty of others?
5. What are the limits of sovereignty?

2

Rights to Self-determination

Introduction

In the Chapter 1, we considered the idea of sovereignty. It is commonly said that states should not normally interfere in the domestic affairs of others in recognition, and in respect, of their sovereignty. Sovereign states should each be able to determine for themselves what future direction they wish to take. Of course, whether they succeed in achieving their aims and purposes is another matter. For example, a state might wish to obtain extra territory or grow its share of the global economy, but these ends require engagement with other states as they are not mere domestic matters and relate to the wider international community.

Before turning to issues of war and distributive justice, the issue of sovereignty raises the question as to whether it is ever divisible with a polity. For example, how might it be possible for a sovereign state to be created from within another sovereign state? This is the issue of whether there are rights to self-determination and, if so, how such rights might work. One way of thinking about this is to consider what, if any, normative justification could be given for any such right. We live in a world of states and where there is a wide variety of ethnic, national, and other groups. So, what could justify a group's right to self-determination and creation of a new state?

And what of the institutional framework relevant to any secession? The breaking off of new states from the old can often come with the breaking

Global Justice: An Introduction, First Edition. Thom Brooks.
© 2023 John Wiley & Sons Ltd. Published 2023 by John Wiley & Sons Ltd.

out of violence and international consequences, from refugees to the recognition of new states by others. How might we understand self-determination in a *realpolitik* world?

This chapter will focus on these two issues – the normative justification of groups to a right to self-determination and the institutional justification of the international context within which secession happens. The discussion aims to clarify what kinds of groups might have a right to self-determination and the international management of this in practice.

Normative justification

In their classic paper, Avishai Margalit and Joseph Raz (1990) focus on this issue.[1] They begin with the importance of groups. The idea of national self-determination is about a group taking control of their future direction. In order to understand any normative justification for national self-determination, we must become clearer about what kind of group could exercise such a right. If we do not, then no such right to self-determination can be made.

We should reflect on the potential boundedness of any group.[2] When we speak of "the people" or "the nation," it is important to think carefully about membership. Who is included – and who is not? Groups can have various things in common. These might include shared tribal membership, ethnic groups, having the same language, religious belief, a common geography, and more. It is not a matter of choosing only one. Often individuals in a group might have two or more of these features in common, such as language and religious beliefs.

The first point to note is the importance of land. Any right to self-determination is about a right to self-govern in some territory. Government requires a space within which to operate and, of course, a boundary within which to exercise sovereignty. It is a necessary feature of a self-determining group, whatever else it is, to share a common territory. In addition, a self-determining group must share this territory with a view to exercising sovereignty over it. It must be more than a common proximity that creates a

---

[1] See *The Global Justice Reader*, chapter 4.

[2] The potential boundedness of groups will raise issues considered later about whether a group might have all of humanity as its membership without any non-members. In discussions of the right to self-determination, it is assumed that groups are bounded with a dividing line – however inexactly drawn – between members and non-members.

group worthy of self-determination. Otherwise, any randomly assembled individuals with no connection beyond their arbitrary location could be sufficient – and such arbitrariness is too weak a connection to bind people in a way that any self-determination as a coherent group might function.

For example, consider an imaginary place called *Random Nation*. This is a group of individuals that have only thing in common: they were each randomly selected to live together in a shared space, spread out across a territory. While grouped together where they live, the individuals in a Random Nation have no other train in common with each other.

Such a collection of people is not a community. Their relations are only arbitrary and virtually anyone else could live here or there in its towns, each as randomly selected as the other. Without any common bond, there are values or aims that individuals could work together and develop in meaningful ways. So, while Random Nation is a kind of group, it is not a kind of group that can have a right to self-determination. Sharing a territory is important, but it does not define a group by itself in any normatively significant way.

Margalit and Raz provide a *normative justification* for the right to self-determination. They argue that – if a group is to have a right to self-determination – this group must share significant normative features. The first is that they must share *a common character* and *culture*. This can take multiple forms, such as sharing a common language, customs, and ceremonies. Margalit and Raz also list having a national food, distinctive architecture, or shared literary and artistic traditions.

The common character and culture of a group is the social glue that holds it together. These kinds of things are deemed normatively important because they are pervasive, displayed across a range of different areas, and of great importance for individuals in that group. While no one feature is necessary – the having or absence of a national food does not make or break a group's possessing a common character – features like these help define the normative significance of a group's *collectivity*, their active collective life.[3] This collectivity can be expressed in multiple ways, such as the flourishing of shared language and expressions or cultural traditions. While difficult to pin any one feature down as a necessary condition for a group to have normative significance, it seems clear that at least having some features are necessary – as, without such features, it might be difficult to distinguish a group having a right to self-determination from Random Nation.

---

[3] The term "collectivity" is mine and not found in Margalit and Raz's work.

Margalit and Raz claim that groups must have a second feature. This is that the tastes of group members are *shaped* by their shared culture. Individuals are, in effect, "marked" by the group's character arising from its collectivity (see Margalit and Raz 1990:444). This does not mean that all members of such a group must think the same or like the same things. No such group exists. Instead, the point is that the common character and culture is pervasive and runs through the group. There is a key link between the individual and their group, recognizing it having normative features as a group.

A third feature of groups highlighted by Margalit and Raz is that group members mutually recognize each other. In addition to group members *having* a connection, they must *see* this connection between themselves and other group members. I must see myself in the group and the group must recognize my inclusion as well. This is a two-way street. I am not a group member if the group does not recognize my membership. Nor, normatively, can I be a member where I do not believe myself included.[4] I must see myself in the group and the group in me, to some extent. Again, this does not require or assume that all members like the same things or think the same way. I can mutually recognize others as conationals even if we support different sports teams, enjoy very different music, and even if we held different views about our group's history.

Finally, the fourth defining feature of a group is that group membership is earned through one's relationship to the group's culture: it is about *belonging* and not personal achievement. For example, I am American not because I wrote this book or obtained a position as professor in the United Kingdom, but because I was born and raised in the United States and a part of its collective life.

Together, these factors create a group identity among a group's members. Margalit and Raz maintain that where groups share these features – they are connected through a common character and culture,

---

[4]This point raises several issues. Legally and politically, I may be a member of a group despite lacking a sense of connection. For example, someone born in the United States but have lived their lives elsewhere may be entitled to American citizenship even if they do not identify themselves as American. The legal possibility is different from the normative connection (or lack of it). Or, I may feel politically alienated from the community that I live in because of a feeling of disconnection, whether through discrimination or inequality. While important, they do not impact Margalit and Raz's arguments as they maintain that members of the group mutually recognize each other as members. Someone who did not identify as a member would not mutually recognize others as comembers of the same collectivity.

individuals are linked with this character and culture, these individuals mutually recognize one another, and their connection is based on relationships – then that group is sufficiently robust normatively to create a normative justification for that group to have a right to self-determine its future for itself.

Importantly, having a right to self-determine does not require that any such group must secede from being a part of a political community with other groups. Just because they can does not mean they must or should.[5] A group may be satisfied with its ability to engage in public affairs and enjoy relative autonomy making breaking away unnecessary and undesirable. Whether or not a group wishes to remain within a larger political community is, at least in part, for that group to decide. Margalit and Raz (1990:457) say "that members of a group are best placed to judge whether their group's prosperity will be jeopardized if it does not enjoy political independence." Ultimately, they claim, "the right to self-determination derives from the value of membership" in a group as Margalit and Raz (1990:456) describe.

There are two final points worth considering further. The first is to reflect on the kind of groups that would not be normatively justified in seceding from a state. Consider the case of Sports Fan Club.[6] This is a group where individuals all support the same sports team, whether it is American football, baseball, or soccer. These individuals have many things in common. They wear the team's merchandize when at games or after work. They sing and cheer their team at matches. They recognize each other as fans either in conversation or by their team clothing.

Sports Fan Club members have a sense of belonging and mutual recognition. But such a club is not the kind of group – as described by Margalit and Raz – that could provide a normative justification for self-determination. For Margalit and Raz, there is no collective, public good at play in supporting a sports team. Nor is belonging centered on the kinds of factors – such as ethnic, national, or religious belonging – that play pervasive roles in the kinds of groups that do have normative significance. Not every club of individuals has that essential, pervasive glue of a shared character and culture that underpins that group as a collectivity, not a mere collection of individuals who happen to enjoy a similar hobby or pastime.

---

[5] It is always important to separate what is possible from what is advisable. Being able to do something does not mean that someone should or must do that thing. For example, having legal or political options is a different matter from having a normative, or moral, reason to do it. They should not be confused and run together.

[6] This example is motivated by Margalit and Raz's (1990) illustration of Tottenham Football Club supporters in English football.

The second point worth considering further is that Margalit and Raz only highlight the essential features for a group that might claim a right to self-determination. In breaking away from a larger political community, there may be further features required, such as an engagement with the wider state. Secession impacts both the group that wants to form a new state and the existing state that may not want to see its territory and population carved out. This is an issue of the institutional justification of self-determination and secession which we will turn to now.

Minimally realist justification

Margalit and Raz focus on the issue of the normative justification of a group's right to self-determination and secede. But it might be argued that this is not the most urgent question, as just alluded to above. The right to self-determination and secession requires an *institutional justification* or otherwise the normative justification remains purely theoretical. This is because secession can often entail conflict and international consequences – and which calls out for a justification of the institutional framework to manage it.

Allen Buchanan (1997:34) makes this argument claiming we need to keep "the institutional question in the foreground."[7] This means, in part, that we must aim to satisfy the condition of "minimal realism" in whatever institutional view we want to justify (Buchanan 1997:42). Minimal realism means having a theory of secession that has a reasonable likelihood of acceptance by existing states under international law. If there is no such chance, then any position taken is unlikely to be realized. This matters for Buchanan because secession is not a merely hypothetical thought experiment about nonexistent people but about actual institutions and real life. Indeed, we might view all political philosophy as having an interest in not only *power* but also the justice of *institutions* through which power might be exercised.

Buchanan considers two different kinds of normative secession theories. The first he calls *primary rights theories*. These are justifications of secession that do not require any underlying injustice. The idea of a primary right is the right is primary: in other words, a group has the right to secede and can do so if – and when – it wants to. This would connect with how Margalit and Raz described groups: whether or not a group has a right to secede depends on the kind of group it is, not how other groups have treated it.

---

[7] See *The Global Justice Reader*, chapter 5.

A second type of normative secession theories are called *remedial right only theories*. This is where secession is justified in relation to some wrong done against a group. Buchanan claims a similar position was held by John Locke, who argued that the people have a right to overthrow their government if, and only if, "their fundamental rights are violated, and more peaceful means have been to no avail" (Buchanan 1997:35; Locke 1980:100–124). Such violations might include the survival of a group's members or their human rights have been threatened, or their previously sovereign state has been unjustly conquered by another. Otherwise, "there is no (general) right to secede from a just state" (Buchanan 1997:37).

Consider there is a community Different Group that lies within the sovereignty of Good State. Assuming the community meets the normative requirements set out by the likes of Margalit and Raz for a right to self-determination, the primary rights theorists would argue that Different Group has the right to secede from Good State – even though the government of Good State treats Different Group members well and without complaint. In contrast, remedial right only theorists argue that while Different Group members may have a clear sense of togetherness, there is no wrong being done to them by Good State and so there is no right to secede.

Compare this with a different situation. Consider the community Different Group instead lives within the sovereignty of Evil State. Different Group members are regularly discriminated against and treated worse than others in Evil State because they are different from Evil State's majority. Again, assuming they meet certain normative requirements for having a right to self-determine generally, both primary rights theorists and remedial rights only theorists would support secession. While they would agree to the same outcome, their reasoning would not be the same. Primary rights theorists would justify secession ill-treatment or not, but remedial right only theorists would argue there is a need for remedy that only secession might secure. So, which kind of theories should we support?

Buchanan defends the remedial right only theorists. Guided by his minimal realism, he argues that a theory of secession ought to be minimally feasible and so consistent with principles of international law, for example. There must be a realistic prospect of a group's secession being recognized as a sovereign state to secure its longer term success. Otherwise, any newly found "independence" will be short-lived. Buchanan (1997:42) is careful to note that his minimal realism is "not a slavish deference" to feasibility. In other words, a justifiable right to secede does not require the guarantee of success. It need only be feasible.

The importance on feasibility drives support for a remedial right only view. This is because the legitimacy of secession to secure a remedy against some fundamental wrongdoing has a more solid basis for global support, in contrast to states that wish to secede for no other reason than they can.

Moreover, for Buchanan, a further attraction of the remedial right only view is that it places significant constraints on secession. He claims this is important because "the majority of secessions have resulted in considerable violence, with attendant large-scale violations of human rights and massive destruction of resources" (Buchanan 1997:44). Therefore, even normatively justified secessions may have serious consequences that should be avoided if possible. This is clearly unavoidable when fundamental rights are threatened or violated. But where there is no wrong nor complaint, the case for secession seems weakened.

What about the parent state?

Thus far, our discussion has focused on the rights of a group – like Different Group – to secede from a larger sovereign state. We have considered the normative justification of a right to self-determination and the minimally realist justification centered on a remedial right only view. We have not considered the duty, if any, of the parent state from which a group secedes. In contrast to the *rights* of groups, what are the *duties* of the parent state?

Let me introduce a simple distinction that will come up in subsequent chapters, too. The distinction is between positive and negative duties. A *positive duty* is where we act when we can. For example, if we saw a child drowning in a pond, we would have a positive duty to rescue if we could save the child.[8] A *negative duty* is where we act to remedy when we have done wrong. For example, if we were responsible for someone drowning, we would have a negative duty to save them. Positive duties are about doing what we can because we can. Negative duties are about doing what we can to fix our wrongs. Now let us apply this distinction to theories of secession.

Consider the community Different Group that lies within the sovereignty of Good State. Let us again assume that Different Group meets the normative requirements for having a right to self-determination. We have seen that only the primary rights theorists would support secession from a state where the group has not been wronged by it. But now let us consider the duties, if any, of the sovereign parent state to Different Group's future secession.

It could be argued that Good State might have a positive duty to support Different Group's secession. This is despite the fact that Good State has

---

[8] See *The Global Justice Reader*, chapter 20.

treated Different Group well and without complaint. If we think we have a positive duty to help realize the rights to self-determination, if Different Group wished to achieve this through secession for any reason, then Good State *might* be under a duty to support Different Group realize this goal. I say they *might* have such a duty and Good State has duties to others, not only Different Group. For example, allowing Different Group to secede might cause harm to Good State by rendering it economically unsustainable. The duties to different groups would need to be considered together. But if this did not apply, then there could be a positive duty to support secession of groups.

Now consider that Different Group lies within Evil State. Not only does Different Group meet the more narrowly stringent test of the remedial right only theorists in seeking secession as a remedy for serious wrongs done to it, it could also be argued that Evil State is under a negative duty to support Different Group's secession on account of Evil State's malign treatment of the group's members. So, not only does Different Group have a right to secede, but also Evil State could be seen to have a duty to support this right.

There is a clear difference between these cases. The positive duty of Good State to support Different Group is weaker than the negative duty of Evil State to do so, as the negative duty is to address a wrong to Different Group. Just as remedial right only theorists have a more stringent right based on addressing a fundamental wrong, so too do states contributing to this wrong to stop and act on their negative duty to address their wrong. The urgency of each right can be weighed intuitively. Most, if not all, of us would say the duty to correct a wrong we have done is more weighty and urgent than a duty to do what we can if we can. The former is more a matter of justice than the latter.

Conclusion

In this chapter, we have considered the right to self-determination and secede. We first reflected on what, if any, normative justification a group might have for secession examining the work of Margalit and Raz. We next examined the minimally realist justification set by Buchanan setting out the importance of feasibility and a defense of a remedial right only view. The discussion sheds light on the kinds of normatively-valuable features any group must have to have such a right to secede, but also to note that this very real practical measure relies, at least in part, in real life acceptance and hence the focus on feasibility.

As we have seen, there may be different views on what rights a group might have to self-determine and secede. But we should take account of the duties of parent states to support such changes. It is claimed that the weightiest account is a negative duty of the parent state to support secession of a group to help rectify the state's wronging that group.

What the discussion has shown is taking a position matters for what is a relevant group, what kind of right it may have to secede, and what variety of duty a parent state might have to support it. Each choice can have significant consequences for all those directly impacted – not least the relevant groups and parent states – but also the global community. Nevertheless, the considerations considered here can help to clarify our thinking about this issue whichever view we prefer.

Discussion questions

1. What is the right to self-determination – and how is it justified?
2. Should only some kinds of groups have a right to self-determination and, if so, why?
3. Why should *Random Nation* not have this right?
4. On what grounds might a group justify secession from another?
5. What duties, if any, does the parent state have to any of its internal groups if a group wanted to secede?

3

Human Rights

Introduction

Human rights are important. Most, if not all, of us would agree that violating someone's human rights is a serious cause for concern. But what is so important about human rights? What is the difference between a right and a *human* right? And how do we know which human rights we have?

This chapter surveys some of the key arguments behind what our human rights are and why – and what is so bad about breaching them. We will consider the origins of the idea of human rights, the United Nation's Declaration of Human Rights as a source of global justification, and the notion of individual and group rights. A common thread running through this discussion is that the idea that fundamental issues of human concern have long been believed to deserve special priority, such as a right to self-preservation or self-defense. What is somewhat less clear is which fundamental issues should receive this priority and why. This chapter will attempt to shed some light on this.

The divine right of kings

Generally speaking, the commonplace view on rights is that individuals only had rights at the discretion of their monarch – and this could be taken away at any time. This view is called *the divine right of kings*. It is most

Global Justice: An Introduction, First Edition. Thom Brooks.
© 2023 John Wiley & Sons Ltd. Published 2023 by John Wiley & Sons Ltd.

famously defended in Sir Robert Filmer's *Patriarcha* (1991:4), who argued that "the greatest liberty in the world ... is for people to live under a monarch." What is special is the divine right that a king has to rule. Filmer (1991:4, 9) says that the first man in the *Bible*, Adam, possessed "lordship ... by creation ... over the whole world" and this divine right to rule human beings is a right that has descended through a "lineal succession." According to Filmer, the rightful kings who rule do so as descendants of Adam and possess his "lordship" over the Earth. For Filmer (1991:12), the king rules his people like a father has power over his family.

The argument for why (absolute) monarchy is the only justified form of government is because, according to Filmer (1991:23), "there is not in scripture mention ... of any other form of government." Therefore, there is no divine support for democracy or other forms of government. Moreover, since there is a divine right of kings, it is for the king to determine rights. Filmer is concerned that the end of liberty will come if all are given the liberty to determine our laws. This is because it will open up societal divisions and factions, as it would create a free-for-all run by individuals who lack divine authority to make such judgements.

I would not expect most, if any, readers to have much sympathy for Filmer's arguments. The idea of individual rights is pervasive, even if still contested, and the divine right of kings is a discredited theory that is of mostly historical interest today.

Nonetheless, it is worth considering some of the devastating critiques the divine right of kings theory has received – as we should not take its rejection for granted because it does not meet with our more modern political sensibilities. The most devastating critique of this classic defence of the divine right of kings is made by John Locke. While political theory student often focuses only on his *Second Treatise of Government*, it is actually in his *First Treatise of Government* where Locke takes aim at Filmer's account with devastating arguments.

For example, Locke says that Filmer's claims are nonsensical. Filmer claims God granted Adam dominion over the world and monarchs, as his descendants, inherit this divine right to rule. Locke points out that Adam, as the first man, is the father of all individuals both princes and paupers. And, if the command to honor one's father and mother is what might ground divine rule, then every father is a king and every mother is a queen – and it is not a position of any one individual (Locke 1988:188). Furthermore, in my favorite criticism, Locke (1988:160) claims that, if Filmer is right, then he should go one step further and claim "that Princes might eat their subjects, too, since God gave as full power to Noah and his heirs to eat *every living thing that moveth*, as he did to Adam to have dominion over them," but of course this is nonsense. So, the idea that there is a divine right of kings descending from Adam and only to kings is illogical and nonsensical on its own terms. There has been no serious defence for this view since Locke's critique.

Natural rights

The main alternative view to the divine right of kings – where rights, if any, were only held conditionally by the grace and favor of the monarch – was the view that individuals held *natural rights*. The key idea is that we possess whatever rights we have *naturally*, and from birth. In other words, we have rights because of who we are – our natural rights are a part of our DNA.

The idea of natural rights raises several important issues. First, natural rights are a part of nature – they are of the world. Defenders of natural rights believed the creator of nature was God and so our natural rights are divinely sanctioned. While this religious aspect does not always play an especially prominent role in most discussions, it is important and easy to overlook. For example, the divine right of kings approach claims that the king has a right to rule because it is the will of God. In contrast, natural rights theorists claim that the will of God is significant, but that this supports the view of individuals having rights irrespective of the monarch's consent.

A second issue is that our rights are naturally a part of us. This means that natural rights are possessed by every human being. Natural rights are held universally. Everyone has natural rights no matter where they live or whatever their citizenship is. Natural rights treats all individuals equally. No one has more of a natural right than anybody else.

A third issue is that natural rights are inalienable. As a natural part of us, natural rights are not features of ourselves that we can shake or cut off.[1] This also means our natural rights are, in effect, pre-political. In other words, we have these rights from entering the world whether or not we are born into a state or an anarchic state of nature. Natural rights are ours to keep and not for any monarch to grant us or take away. Our rights are a legitimate constraint on political authority as no government should violate the natural rights of its citizens.

---

[1] Some classical natural rights theorists claim that – as natural rights are sanctioned by God – anyone who tries to violate the natural rights of themselves or others is answerable to God, as he/she would act contrary to God's command.

But the fourth issue is that natural rights theorists disagree about which natural rights we have – in both their content and number. For example, Thomas Hobbes argues there is only one natural right while John Locke claims there are three. Hobbes (1996:91) says the only natural right we have is a right to self-preservation. While in an anarchic state of nature where we are constantly under threat from others, he claims we would each seek the security of living in a state. Hobbes claims we each endeavor toward peace, but remain in a state of war until this peace is obtained. He argues we would each give up our "rights to all things" and join with others in creating a sovereign state (Hobbes 1996:92). We surrender our liberty to secure our self-preservation and enjoy our natural right.

In contrast, Locke (1988:271) argues we all have more natural rights than Hobbes claims. For Locke, we all have a natural right to "life, liberty and property." (The American founding fathers relabeled these rights as about "life, liberty and the pursuit of happiness.")[2] For Locke, our right to self-preservation is no less important than to our liberty or enjoyment of property, as each needs the other. So, while natural rights theorists agree that there are natural rights, they disagree about what they are – and such lists could be drawn up very differently by different people, with each claiming the right(s) in question naturally belong to any individual.

But there is a deeper criticism some have raised. Natural rights theorists, like Hobbes and Locke, claim natural rights are *natural*. Peter Jones (1994:79) argues:

> Trees, bees and buttercups are all parts of nature, so, on this view it would seem, are rights. We cannot doubt the existence of tress, bees and buttercups, nor, it would seem, can we doubt the existence of rights. Yet rights clearly do not "exist" in the same manifest way as these other things … Not unreasonably, therefore, natural rights theorists have been accused of trying to pass off a highly questionable moral notion as though its presence in the universe were a matter of fact.

Jones highlights the question begging nature of natural rights. The claim that a right to property exists *because it is natural* makes several unstated assumptions. First, it assumes that rights are as natural as the birds and the bees while existing very differently: we can see bird species, but do not know rights in the same way. Secondly, natural rights theorists assume that because rights are natural they therefore hold a special, positive status to mark out our fundamental interests. However, not everything natural is

---

[2] See US Declaration of Independence, 1776.

positive, such as poison ivy, viruses, such as COVID, or cancer. Each begs the question of why natural rights should be recognized: it is unsatisfactory to simply point to their being natural by definition. What we need is a justification that spells out this importance rather than only assume it.

What is a right?

As we have seen, natural rights theorists disagree with themselves about how many rights there are – and many of us might disagree with their views on how these rights are justified. This raises the issue of what are rights, if not natural rights, and how are they justified?

Perhaps the first thing to notice are the kinds of things we might consider rights to be – and how the way we use rights-talk (e.g. the way we talk about rights) sees rights pursuing different ends.[3] For example, one way of thinking about rights is to be exempt from usual duties. Citizens cannot break into a home to handcuff someone, but a police officer can when chasing a suspect and making an arrest (Wenar 2005:226). Citizens cannot simply operate a car without possessing a driver's license first either. The rights of the police to arrest or citizens to drive a car on a license are ways in which rights confer *privileges* in exempting individuals from usual duties. In addition, these rights as privileges also convey discretion. The police officer may call for a colleague to give pursuit instead – or I may choose not to drive a car, although I could if desired, on my license. In these ways, rights as privileges can be used to provide an exemption from normal duties and discretion about doing so. Having the right does not require that I exercise it.

A second way of thinking about rights is as a *claim*. For instance, I might claim a right to not be physically harmed by others. My claimed right functions as a source of protection. Or an employee might claim a right to their pay. The claimed right serves to demand some kind of specific performance from others.

We can think about rights in a third way as a *power*. This form of rights is about altering our privileges and claims – as well as ensuring our privileges and claims are not altered by others (Wenar 2005:230–231). For example, suppose Bill has a large fortune. Bill has no duty to share it. Nor do others have a right to it. But suppose Bill chooses to promise his fortune to Betsy. If he does, Bill creates a claim for Betsy to his fortune – and, correspondingly, Bill creates a duty for himself to make good on his promise to Betsy. This is one way that rights might alter claims.

---

[3] See *The Global Justice Reader*, chapter 7.

Or suppose a judge must decide sentencing for a convicted criminal (Wenar 2005:231). The judge has the power to sentence because they have the right to do so. If the crime carries a mandatory sentence, then the judge has only the power to enforce this sentence – and, in so doing, prevent the criminal from enjoying free movement outside prison walls. But if the crimes do not have a mandatory punishment, the judge can exercise discretion in what we might call a paired power granting them the power to waive (or not to waive) time in prison, instead of issuing community service. In these ways, a right is a power that can alter the privileges and claims on others.

A fourth, and final, way we might think about rights is as an *immunity*. For example, Americans have protected free speech as enshrined in the US Constitution. They have an immunity from the government's infringement of this right. Most citizens have rights against cruel and unusual punishment arising from either national law or the Universal Declaration of Human Rights. This, too, provides individuals with an immunity to overly severe or unnecessary sentencing (see Brooks 2023b).

This discussion has identified four different kinds of rights (e.g. powers, claims, privileges, and immunities) that can have one or more of several different functions, such as exemptions, discretion, protection, and performance. The four different kinds of rights are also sometimes referred to "Hohfeldian incidents" – or as incidents of rights – named for Wesley Hohfeld (1919), who originally developed this framework. As Leif Wenar (2005:246) points out in his careful study of Hohfeld's framework, it shows us that "rights" are not of one thing, of a single kind or function. We would be mistaken to think that all rights act the same way and reject a monist conception. There are different kinds of rights and this framework helps us understand their varieties.

So, all rights fall into one of these four kinds (or Hohfeldian incidents), such as powers, claims, privileges, or immunities. The next issue is whether all such incidents are rights. Consider the case of an immunity. A university does not have any power to grant citizenship to students. The student could be said to have an immunity against their university awarding them citizenship. Yet, it would be odd – and perhaps somewhat nonsensical – to say that the students have a *right* that their university does not grant them citizenship. (Indeed, the right to grant citizenship is with the state – so it has a location, only not with universities.) This is case where there is a kind of right (or incident) that fails to map onto an appropriately fitting function, namely, the immunity in question does not provide a protection. Not all incidents are rights (but all rights are incidents). What is required is that incidents must connect with one of the several different functions noted above, such as exemptions, discretion, protection, and performance amongst others.

What is a human right

There is rights-talk about "rights" and "human rights," but what is the difference? Human rights set out minimal standards of "high priority norms" that are universally inclusive of all individuals (Nickels 2007:9–10). They can come in the form of "security rights" such as life, liberty, and security of person and a prohibition on torture of cruel punishments or in the form of "economic and social rights" such as rights to education or health care, for example (Nickels 2007:11; UNDP 1948). As standards to be met, and not merely ideals beyond our reach, they impose significant constraints on governments in terms of their policy-making, law-making, and official behavior. Charles Beitz (2001) describes human rights as a kind of common concern shared internationally across political communities.[4] As a common concern, any conception of human rights should aspire to gain the broadest possible support. But at the same time, human rights are not normatively neutral. Beitz (2001:274) claims we should not expect or require that "they are necessarily either accepted by or acceptable to everyone" as there will be great diversity in political and ethical beliefs worldwide and we should not expect that everyone must always be in full agreement about what is a human right.

One common way of thinking about human rights is our basic needs, such as the kinds of rights that Locke lists like rights to life, liberty, and property that concern the security of ourselves physically and socially.[5] These needs identify a "global minimum" that everyone is entitled to as a matter of justice, imposing obligations on their governments (Miller 2007:166). Needs highlight what is essential rather than what is optional signifying greater moral urgency and a more "substantive moral view" (Miller 1976:122). There is more weight given to what is a need than what is not – and to be deprived of a need is therefore considered a greater wrong (Miller 2007:181). But what is essential is to determine what is actually necessary for people to lead decent lives wherever they live – and not, according to David Miller (2007:184), "what people in those cultures may

---

[4] This chapter is included in only the first edition of *The Global Justice Reader*, chapter 8.

[5] Some of the language used about needs can be confusing. For example, Miller distinguishes between "basic needs" and "societal needs" which might suggest that the former is absent rights relating to social justice. But he is explicit that this is not the case. Instead, "basic needs" are needs for anyone to have a decent life in any society whereas "societal needs" is seen as a more expansive list reflecting cultural norms and practices of a particular society (see Miller 2007:182–183). So, basic needs can include social needs, but societal needs are exclusively concerned with non-universal needs.

believe is necessary" from a merely subjective point of view. This focus on basic needs is seen as the way to decide what are our human rights, and the special status such rights deserve.

A second way to think about human rights is to claim they are our fundamental capabilities "to do or be" (Nussbaum 2003; see Nussbaum 2000).[6] For example, Martha C. Nussbaum argues there are ten human capabilities: life; bodily health; bodily integrity; senses, imagination and thought; emotions; practical reason; affiliation; other species; play and control over one's environment (Nussbaum 2011:33–34).[7] Each capability is of central importance and equal in weight to any other. The idea is that a decent life is where our capability to do or be in any of the listed areas is open to us. We are able to live a life worth living, be adequately nourished in good health, and to have attachments to other people. Governments have a duty to ensure we are each able to enjoy any capability above a threshold. In other words, every state must ensure that individuals enjoy a decent life across these areas above a certain level. If not, our human rights are breached.

The differences between these views can appear somewhat small. Both mark out a minimal set of essential goods that should be protected. One difference is that capabilities can be more flexibly applied. While everyone must have their capability to bodily health secured, it is for local communities to decide how this universal standard is reached, say, through a national health service or an alternative. In contrast, the basic needs approach opposes realizing the same need in different ways. A second difference is that basic needs are essential and so seemingly inalienable. On the contrary, the capabilities approach is about freedom. It is essential my capability to do something, such as engage in social interaction, is secured for me, but not required that I actually choose to perform any capability – of course, raising its own concern about how essential any one element is if I could choose to go without (Brooks 2014a).[8]

---

[6] This article is included in only the first edition of *The Global Justice Reader*, chapter 34.

[7] Nussbaum's capabilities approach develops from pioneering work by Amartya Sen (1993, 1999, see Brooks 2015b). We will consider capabilities further in chapters 7 and 10.

[8] It might also be argued that some kinds of capabilities (such as those concerning the body like life or bodily health) are more fundamental than others (such as "brain"-related capabilities like senses, imagination and thought or "boundaries"-related capabilities like affiliation or play). This view is consistent with the position that all capabilities are fundamental rights, but that some carry greater weight or importance than others (Brooks 2020c).

Whichever view we find compelling, human rights as fundamentally speaking to what governments must do to address serious kinds of problems with global reach. For example, my cell phone's battery might die while travelling. This could certainly cause a problem for me if I should be delayed or become lost. But it is hardly a serious enough problem requiring a global remedy. On the contrary, the possibility of being tortured is a serious problem for everyone, as it can terrorize or cause severe harm.

Moreover, human rights are often incorporated in our laws. They are not merely an aspiration or normatively compelling, but a part of our positive law and enforceable. This is true both locally and globally, as human rights can be enshrined in a country's law and in international law. In these ways, human rights have a concrete existence – or materiality – that other kinds of rights may lack.

Human rights can be the subject of international consensus. For example, the *Universal Declaration of Human Rights* (UNDR) is an important milestone adopted by the United Nations' General Assembly in 1948.[9] Its provisions include human rights to everyone being born free and equal, a right to "life, liberty and security of person" and the prohibition of slavery, cruel or degrading punishments, and torture. There are rights to receive a free education and to freely participate in the cultural life of their community – and many more. The UNDR is therefore wide-ranging. It enshrines natural rights (such as the right to life) with social rights (like the right to a free education) covering what we might consider basic needs, social needs, and fundamental capabilities. The UNDR is very much what it says that it is: a *universal* declaration of *human rights*, a practical illustration of where there has been and remains broad, international agreement about what our human rights are – and setting out the minimum standards that all governments must respect (see Miller 2007:164).

The UNDR is a useful example of human rights, setting a threshold that every government should protect and maintain. As a minimal standard, some philosophers, like James Nickel, argue that this is constructive. It allows us to both protect essential human interests while not becoming overly prescriptive about how to do so – and so allows a crucial space for states to exercise their right to self-determine their laws in their own ways. [10] This would help further the political aim of ensuring as many countries as possible to adopt the same standard with this ability to contextualize the realization of human rights for their society, not unlike the adaptability noted above with the capabilities approach.

---

[9] See *The Global Justice Reader*, chapter 6.
[10] See *The Global Justice Reader*, chapter 8.

Do groups have rights?

So far, we have only considered the human rights of *individuals*, but not *groups*. The most influential view of groups rights is developed by Peter Jones (1999).[11] The idea of group rights might seem mistaken. In the controversial words of former British Prime Minister Margaret Thatcher, "there is no such thing as society" – only the individual exists. So, how might groups have rights?

Group rights are rights that individuals only possess together, and not individually on their own. We do speak of rights as groups, such as a group's right to self-determination as seen in Chapter 2. The individuals in a group have such a right as a particular group. This is different from, for example, saying religious believers can practice their religion as the right to religious freedom is a right that can be enjoyed individually. Group rights are rights that can only be enjoyed as a collective.

Jones argues that group members must have some kind of shared identity as a group. This common connection can give rights to groups. For example, individuals identify themselves as members of a collective nation or tribe. It is common to say that a territory or tract of land belongs – not to any specific individual, but – to the nation or tribe. This is an example of a group right. These rights matter, too, for a state, its natural resources and much more.

For Jones, group rights come in two varieties. The first is the *collective* conception. This is where a group shares in a joint interest that can ground a right, such as the maintenance of a culture or way of life. A second form is the *corporate* conception. This is where a group has a right qua its being a group rather than to its individual members, even if no central joint interest. Jones claims we need not choose a side as neither is exclusive of the other, as group rights might be found to be best justified in relation to one or the other. This is an issue we will return to in Chapter 4 on nationalism.

Rights violations

If human rights signify an essential interest to be protected, then their breach should be considered a serious concern. Human rights mark out important limits. Yet, enforcing the crucial line between rights-compliance and rights-violations can be challenging. For example, rights often come

---

[11] See *The Global Justice Reader*, chapter 9. See Jones (1994:182–187).

with responsibilities. A right to free speech is not a right to speak however freely someone might like. There are limits on exercising rights, such as not to defame through spreading falsehoods or using words – like shouting "fire!" in a crowded theatre – that could endanger others.

Torture is routinely singled out as an example of a human rights violation. The use of torture involves the intentional use of violence, fear, and cruelty (Wisnewski 2010). But can it ever be justified in extreme circumstances, such as the fight on the "war on terror"?

Philosophers argue for both sides (Miller 2017). Consider the Case of the Ticking Time Bomb:

A terrorist has hidden a ticking time bomb somewhere in a major city. If the bomb explodes, it will kill thousands of innocent people. Only the terrorist knows where the bomb is hidden. Only if tortured, he would identify where the bomb is hidden so its timer would be turned off in time to save lives.

Many consequentialists might support the use of torture in this case. The torture of one individual to save the lives of many thousands may seem like a price worth paying for the best possible circumstances. Utilitarians maximizing overall pleasure and seeking to minimize overall pain would find the pain to the individual tortured far less than the pleasure to the thousands whose lives would be saved. Non-consequentialists might claim that such actions are wrong irrespective of their consequences.

What is noticeable about examples like the Case of the Ticking Time Bomb are the qualifications: thousands *will* die, *only* the terrorist knows where the bomb is hidden and *only* if tortured would the terrorist share this information and *in time* to save lives. It could be objected that if all of these qualifications must obtain to justify torture in theory, they are implausible and unlikely to happen in practice. For instance, how do we know there is no CCTV or witnesses to the terrorist hiding the bomb that could be used to locate it? Or why assume, if tortured, the terrorist would confess truthfully? We might imagine that someone put in severe pain might say or do anything to make it stop, even if confessing to something they did not do. Or we could expect someone who is tortured to be less reliable because of the severity of the pain would impair their ability to think and share correct information (O'Mara 2015). So, even if persuaded by the narrow qualifications of a hypothetical example, this is far enough removed from real world examples that more justificatory work is required.

And so we might respond with a simple "no" that torture is always wrong. Intentionally inflicting cruelty on others is morally repugnant, it could be argued, and beyond the pale for any just government to impose. This position is adopted internationally, too. It is a clear violation of the UDHR and the United Nations Convention against Torture and Other Cruel, Inhuman or Degrading Treatments or Punishment adopted by the United Nation in 1984. But it is noteworthy that while there is a prohibition against torture, there is not a similar ban on other serious forms of punishment like the death penalty. This raises the question of why torture might be different.

David Sussman (2005) offers an interesting response to this question.[12] He argues that torture is not only morally objectionable because of its cruelty, but as "a kind of forced self-betrayal" (Sussman 2005:28). This refers to the uses of torture where their victim is an active participant in their own abuse. Examples include the denial of access to toilet facilities to force victims to soil themselves as they struggle in vain not to do so. Or to stand or maintain contorted positions for prolonged periods or the use of partial drownings.

Each puts the victim in "the hopeless struggle" against their own natural urges for rest or to breath (Sussman 2005:22–23). The torture victim is both helpless at the hands of his interrogators and an active participant in his suffering, coerced to take part in the cruel ritual. Thus, the victim's autonomy is not merely violated, but perverted in the act of his being tortured. Torture is never justifiable, but Sussman's point is that this is perhaps for even more reasons than we might normally think.

Conclusion

While the idea of rights has a long history, it has been understood in very different ways, such as a divine right of kings, natural rights, or human rights. Each attempts to express something of fundamental, timeless importance worthy of respect and moral urgency. There is global support for universal rights as recognized by examples like the UDHR, but there remain challenges in ensuring that the lines drawn by human rights are clearly set out, widely shared and properly enforced.

This chapter has surveyed some of the leading ideas behind what rights are and understandings about what makes human rights different. It has considered the issue of how we might understand group rights and the importance of limits. Rights are a complex area and there is much more to

---

[12] See *The Global Justice Reader*, chapter 10.

say about different perspectives on their foundation as well as their content, but it is hoped the reader will have a sufficient familiarity to explore the philosophy of rights further.[13]

Discussion questions

1. What is the difference between natural rights and human rights?
2. Why are human rights important?
3. How do we know what are our human rights?
4. Should human rights be understood the same way in every community – or can there be different ways of understanding them?
5. Are violations of human rights, such as torture, especially wrong – and, if so, how?

---

[13] See further reading Beitz (2009), Jones (1994), and Cruft, Liao, and Renzo (2015).

4

Nationalism and Patriotism

Introduction

We do not choose where we are born. Our citizenship at birth is determined arbitrarily, at least from the infant's perspective.[1] One issue is whether this matters morally. While our being a national of a particular place might have arisen arbitrarily, does this mean our national ties are morally arbitrary? How might our shared citizenship give rise to duties between conationals? And how might we understand patriotism in this context?

This chapter surveys key contributions to our thinking about nationalism and patriotism. Work in this area focuses on how our shared identity as a group has normative significance and how this is justified. It also highlights the value of patriotism and the socio–political connections we have with others in our group. These ideas will be contrasted with cosmopolitanism in the Chapter 5 – this is the main alternative to nationalism.

---

[1] It is worth noting that an infant's nationality might not be arbitrary from the parents' perspective(s). For example, they might wish, if they are able to choose, to create conditions whereby their child can possess a particular nationality. An example is some countries, like the United States or the Republic of Ireland, may grant citizenship to individuals born there. While an infant does not choose, their parent might and so birth right citizenship is arbitrary for the former but perhaps not always for the latter.

Global Justice: An Introduction, First Edition. Thom Brooks.

Classical nationalism

It is essential to set out two forms of nationalism. The first might be called *classical nationalism* (Miscevic 2020). This is the idea that all individuals are members of a *nation* that is defined by sharing some common origin, ethnicity, or cultural ties. An individual's national membership is generally involuntary and a product of birth. Historically many states might have been organized as *nation-states* where the state's members all shared the same national connection.

The classical nationalism model is often criticized for its grounding duties for its members in their arbitrary connection as an ethno-cultural group. Such bonds lack normative justification. For example, political philosophers like John Rawls (1996:133–172) argued that nationalism based on race was an unreasonable view of the good that could not play a part in constructing a just society. Such nationalists fail to acknowledge the fact of reasonable diversity in any society and cannot support political stability over time. This is because they do not acknowledge the salience of different views of the good (Brooks 2015b:167).

Classical nationalism is also criticized by some for contributing to conflict and war. Of course, wars have been fought before there were nation-states or nationalism (Hall and Malesevic 2013). Nonetheless, any view that fellow nationalists ought to forge a nation free from nonmember interference will open up risks of division and antagonism. It raises the issue of whether establishing identities of "us" and "them" can be ethically justified or if it might contribute to an avoidable risk of future conflict. More extreme versions, such as *fascism*, seek to rid the society of any unofficial view in the name of unity, sometimes backed by the threat and use of violence. Such views should have no role to play in governing nor public policy more generally as so unreasonable as to be toxic.

Liberal nationalism

A second form of nationalism might be called *liberal nationalism* (Brock 2009:248–273).[2] This is the view of nations as "ethical communities" (Miller 1999:49).[3] These are groups of individuals who share a connection with ethical significance. Miller (1999:65) says:

---

[2] This position is sometimes referred to as "ethical nationalism" or "anticosmopolitanism." I retain its most common usage as liberal nationalism above.
[3] This chapter is included in only the first edition of *The Global Justice Reader*, chapter 14.

Because I identify with my family, my college, or my local community, I properly acknowledge obligations to members of these groups that are distinct from the obligations I owe to people generally. Seeing myself as a member, I feel a loyalty to the group, and this expresses itself, among other things, in my giving special weight to the interests of fellow-members.

This view connects with what was seen earlier about groups having a right to self-determination. When individuals have an identity forged from sharing a common character and culture, this can have normative weight. Not every group will possess such an identity, such as a Random Nation of individuals grouped together arbitrarily. But groups where individuals identify with their shared character and culture are neither arbitrary nor random and may give rise to duties between members of a group as group members.

It is important to recognize that boundaries matter for liberal nationalism, but not in the usual sense. Liberal nationalists care only for the ethical boundaries around a group of people. Territorial boundaries are usually seen as proxies for where these lines can be drawn, but – as ethical – the border is drawn around the ethical boundary rather than by any territorial features, such as coastlines or rivers (Goodin 1988).[4] Metaphorically speaking, the ethical glue, so to speak, that holds groups together as an ethical community is their shared identity and not necessarily their relative geographical proximity – although, of course, sharing a territory can be a helpful proxy for demarcating an ethical nation's sovereignty, but only inexactly. To emphasize, liberal nationalism's boundaries are people-centric, not geography-centric.

It is because liberal nationalists argue that borders are fundamentally around people that they speak of the *nation* as the ethical group – and not the state. While we might think the nation or the state are generally synonymous in everyday talk, there is a crucial difference. States have land borders whereas nations do not, as the border encircles members. In focusing on nations (and not states), liberal nationalists draw attention to the group as bounded as an ethical community rather than as a territory, as with a state.

A central distinction used by political philosophers is between general and specific duties. *General duties* are what we would have to everyone and so have universal application. These duties treat all human beings equally.

---

[4] This chapter is included in only the first edition of *The Global Justice Reader*, chapter 13.

In contrast, *special associative duties* are what we would owe to particular individuals because of some special – and specific – relation we have to them.[5] These duties could give recognition to compatriots as our compatriots, or to our family members as our family.

For Miller, it is *not* the case that any special duties I might have toward my compatriots always trumps my general duties to all individuals, both compatriots and non-compatriots. Consider the following Case of Children in Need:

> There are two children drowning in a pond. We are able to wade over to the children, but only have time to choose one child to rescue.

How could we choose? We have a general duty to everyone. Let us assume that both children are unconnected and unknown to us. Would we flip a coin to choose whom to save? Our general duty to each is equal and both have the same claim for rescue.

Reconsider the example so that one of the drowning children is connected to us. If we have time to save only one, we would all act to save the child who was ours or a family member's. In fact, we would likely say that someone who did not choose to save their own child would have committed a serious wrong.

The issue is how far the moral relevance of such connectedness might extend. Consider similarly where two individuals are in equally urgent need and you have a connection to only one of them. Some factors clearly have no normative weight. If only one has the same hair color (or bald) like me or happens to have the same favorite color, these arbitrary factors are irrelevant.

But it is different if what we have in common is that we are conationals. This connection is ethical. Co-nationals have a shared character and culture as members of the same group. This connection creates *associative duties* between group members that they have to one another (Seglow 2010). Group members have various duties to other members that they do not have to non-group members. They hold their governments to account, follow their laws, pay taxes, sit on juries, serve in the armed forces and much more.

Co-nationals have these additional duties as members of a national group. They do not have the same duties to members abroad. Our membership of a national group creates special associative duties to group members that *supplement*, but not replace or downgrade, our general duties to all. We may

---

[5] "Special associative duties" are sometimes referred to as "special duties."

act on our associative duties to conationals so long as we respect the general duties we have toward all. Consider the Revised Case of Children in Need:

> There are two children asking for help. One child is drowning and the second child is completing homework. The second child is a co-national. We only have time to help one child.

Both children have claims, but the first child's claim has more moral urgency. Our general duties are greater to this child even if we also had an additional associative duty to the second child, as a conational, because the second child's claim is far less urgent. The example illustrates that liberal nationalists can recognize associative duties supplementing general duties while honoring general duties.[6]

There might be an objection that group membership does not create special duties. For example, few of us choose our nationality. Where we are a citizen is as given to us as the natural color of our hair and arbitrarily determined for us. No one chose where to be born.

But while our nationality at birth might be arbitrary, our being a national is not. It is not something that only happens to me – like being right-handed or color-blind. Our nationality is a more substantive part of us. Nationality informs our rights and duties. Our nationality is often recognized as a protected characteristic to safeguard against discrimination. This is not true of having a certain hair color or being right or left-handed. Nationality matters in a way that those other features do not. Moreover, it is as conationals that we might pursue a right to self-determination. Groups based on arbitrary connections have no such right and give rise to no associative duties. We might not choose our birth nationality, but our group membership is an important aspect of ourselves with ethical substance and consequences.

National identity can have importance for a political community. This is captured well by the multicultural theorist Bhikhu Parekh (2008:59–60):

> The identity of a political community consists of those constitutive features that define and distinguish it from others and make it *this* community rather than some other. It includes its territory, . . . language or languages, and formative historical experiences, including those surrounding its origins in terms of which it traces its development. It also

---

[6] It would be objectionable if liberal nationalists weighed general duties to all individuals *less* than associative duties to conationals. This would mean not treating everyone the same up to a threshold – an issue explored further in the next chapter.

includes its traditions, deep-seated tendencies, beliefs, values and ideals that it cherishes and seeks to cultivate in its members, the discursive framework and the style of reasoning that characterize its ways of debating and resolving differences, its legal and political institutions in terms of which it organizes its affairs and relates to other communities, and the collective memories of internal and external struggles, triumphs and defeats.[7]

Our national identity is a narrative of its members about the community's character, its values, and sense of belonging. It is a self-understanding about the past, present, and future of that community as part of a national story that is continually refreshed and revised.[8] Identities are complex, multi-layered, contains sometimes conflicting strains of thought and it "exists" insofar as its members see themselves as part of it. As Parekh (2019:65) rightly observes, we support our state and its laws not simply because of weighing up reasons or reflecting on consent, but because we "identify with and care for it."

Nationalism without nations

Liberal nationalism focuses on the national group. But it raises the issue of whether only membership in a national group counts, or whether we can have associative rights and duties through other forms of group membership. We have other intrinsically valuable shared identities that have moral significance – and that do not compel us to give less to those for whom we have general duties – beyond the nation (Brooks 2014b).

For example, organized religions are groups that can create ethical duties and responsibilities for its members like nations can for their members. Religious organizations are structured communities of believers joined together in a shared identity and communal project. Religious organizations have an identifiable public culture that often crosses national boundaries. Believers place great value in both their faith as well as their membership in their religious community. They have a shared group identity that has intrinsic value and entails a recognized responsibility among its members – all of which is like the kinds of ethically valuable groups that

---

[7] Emphasis added.

[8] See Parekh (2008:60): "Members of a political community seek to make sense of it and its history, from a general conception of the kind of community it is, and arrive at some form of self-understanding."

individuals have as members of a nation. And to underscore that liberal nationalism might extend beyond nations to group identities like religious organizations, it is noteworthy to highlight that these organizations not only have their own rights and responsibilities for those in the group but also often their own form of laws.

The consequences for this position is that the nation, or state, are not the only groups that have rights and duties in the international sphere. Our connection to others as conationals is important, but it is not the only way that we can create associative duties between group members. It highlights the importance of a group's shared identity for liberal nationalism which can be applied to other forms of ethically relevant group identities. So, if liberal nationalists are right about the importance of the kind of group identity found in the national group for global justice, they should recognize non-national groups who share the same kind of group identities for global justice. Global justice is not only for nations, but also for other kinds of groups where the intrinsic value of group membership works in the same way.[9]

Patriotism and cosmopolitanism

One possible objection is that liberal nationalists have a "patriotic bias" toward their compatriots and over distant others. The objection is that their associative duties give extra weight to their local group. Richard W. Miller (1998) considers this alleged bias in relation to the commonly expressed view that affluent countries should put a greater priority on their own interests first at home than in supporting others abroad.[10] This is unsurprising if we consider patriotism's roots as a "love of country" and the value patriots give to a country they see as theirs with a sense of belonging (Jones and Vernon 2018:11).

Miller defends a position similar to what is outlined above. He accepts that we can and should have patriotic concern for our conationals. But this need not mean a lack of concern for others elsewhere outside our state. We have general duties to all and special associative duties to those in our community, but where the latter supplement the former and viewed in context. Miller (1998:220) says:

---

[9] This issue returns in Chapter 7 when considering what agents – whether the state or other bodies – can have duties to individuals in severe poverty.
[10] See *The Global Justice Reader*, chapter 12.

In a morality of equal *concern* for all, this higher cost of living decently would tend to reduce the amount of provision for the worst-off of per-capita rich countries, since provision for the poor in per-capita poor countries more efficiently satisfies needs.

If our concern is to provide support for all, less aid might go further in promoting well-being in per-capita poor countries than the more affluent. This does not mean we should avoid supporting the destitute in our own state at all. But it is to say that recognizing special associative duties of compatriots should not make us ignore the support needed elsewhere. It may even be in our interest, in terms of advancing an equal concern for all, to be active in international aid addressing general duties to those in more urgent need alongside principled, yet pragmatic, factors.

A related issue to the Patriotic Bias Objection is that, it might be argued, liberal nationalists are unable to connect with non-compatriots in a meaningful way. In choosing a patriotic love of the group, they are unable to become a cosmopolitan citizen of the world. They should direct their celebration of national unity around "worthy moral goals of justice and equality" that connects "the worldwide community of human beings" (Nussbaum 2002:2).

This issue is considered by Martha Nussbaum (2002). She rightly points out that an allegiance to supporting our state could contribute to our defending unjustified privilege.[11] She argues that we – the citizens of affluent Western countries – should be troubled by global inequality between rich and poor countries and the damaging environmental impact of West. Our support for our particular group – and its place in an unequal world – might be thought antithetical from being dedicated toward supporting a more just world order.

Moreover, a priority of the more immediate or personal identities could distance us further from attachments with those more distant. For example, I might claim to be an American first and world citizen second, but I could quickly learn to say that I am of a religious or class background first and American second – which would only serve to distance us even further.

Some might say that we face a choice between being a citizen of somewhere or of everywhere – and to adopt one is to reject the other. And, of course, we have attachments to those who are near and dear, including our families, neighbors, and friends. It might appear that to have a greater

---

[11] See *The Global Justice Reader*, chapter 11.

regard for distant others elsewhere that we might need to compromise or somehow constrain our regard for those we know and love.

Nussbaum argues that there is no such choice to be made. She argues:

> The Stoics stress that to be a citizen of the world one does not need to give up local identifications, which can be a source of great richness in life. They suggest that we think of ourselves not as devoid of local affiliations, but as surrounded by a series of concentric circles. The first one encircles the self, the next takes in the immediate family, then follows the extended family, then, in order, neighbors or local groups, fellow city-dwellers, and fellow countrymen – and we can easily add to this list groupings based on ethnic, linguistic, historical, professional, gender, or sexual identities. Outside all these circles is the largest one, humanity as a whole. Our task as citizens of the world will be to "draw the circles somehow toward the centre". (Nussbaum 2002:9)[12]

This extended passage shows a clear pathway through patriotism to cosmopolitanism (and the topic of Chapter 5). Our shared identities with those who are close to us are not a block to developing a wider concern to encompass all of humanity, but a first step in this direction. It is through our developing ever widening shared identities with family, neighbors, and compatriots that we expand our circles of concern ever more widely.

Becoming a citizen of the world is not to deny who we are or where we are from. It is from a grounding in our particular identities that we can transform ourselves and extend ourselves further. It is through our patriotism that can lead us to a higher "allegiance to what is morally good – and that which, being good, I can command as such to all human beings" (Nussbaum 2002:2).

Conclusion

Nationalism can often be thought about in a classical way linked to a particular people. As we have seen, nationalism can be defended in a different way based on an ethical foundation. Individuals can have membership in ethically relevant groups. Our group membership is important as it can create special associative duties between individual members.

Liberal nationalists do not argue that these special duties trump our general duties to all. The morally urgent needs of others take precedence regardless of nationality. But what nationalists argue is that our shared

---

[12] Nussbaum quotes the Stoic Hierocles.

identity as compatriots can matter ethically in terms of the rights and duties we have toward one another that supplement our general duties. Where all else is equal, our sharing group membership might justify choosing compatriots over others.

The name "liberal nationalists" might suggest that the view only applied to "nations." However, the ethical-relevance of groups can apply to both nations and nonnations, such as religious organizations. We can have a kind of nationalism without nations. Moreover, it is through our shared identities in various connections as friends, families and more that not only connects us to our individual group, but which serves as a foundation for a more global identity – the likes of which we will consider in the following chapter.

Discussion questions

1. Does our shared membership in a group matter for ethical decisions?
2. What reason, if any, could justify treating some people differently than others?
3. Which kind(s) of identity can create special associative duties?
4. What is the difference between general and special duties – and how do they compare?
5. How is it possible to be a patriot and world citizen?

5

Cosmopolitanism

Introduction

Cosmopolitanism is about the moral equality of human beings. Every individual deserves the same concern and equal respect – each person is "the ultimate unit of moral concern and to be entitled to equal consideration regardless of nationality and citizenship" (Tan 2004:1; see Held 2010). None of us chooses our nationality at birth. It is morally arbitrary that we are born into one community and not another. Cosmopolitans argue broadly that these arbitrary circumstances should not undermine the equality of every individual. As morally equal, we should have the same access to rights and general well-being. This should not be a matter of being lucky to have been born into a more wealthy community than a poorer one – as this arbitrary difference is a matter of injustice.

Cosmopolitanism is the main alternative to liberal nationalists. While the latter focus on the justification of permitting *different* duties and obligations from special associative duties created from group membership, cosmopolitans focus instead on the *general* duties and obligations we all have as human beings.

In this chapter, we will explore the historical roots of modern cosmopolitanism in the work of Immanuel Kant. While he stops short of advocating a world government, Kant claims that a cosmopolitan world order makes possible a future of peace without conflict. Next we consider how his

Global Justice: An Introduction, First Edition. Thom Brooks.
© 2023 John Wiley & Sons Ltd. Published 2023 by John Wiley & Sons Ltd.

cosmopolitan ideals fit with notions of patriotism and global equality of opportunity – with echoes of what we saw in Nussbaum's argument for how patriotism can help foster a grounded cosmopolitanism. Finally, we will reflect on how cosmopolitan thought could be reframed in a way unbounded to any one tradition in a more "global" global philosophy. Each takes us deeper into what it means to take the moral equality of individuals seriously as a matter for global justice.[1]

Cosmopolitan justice

Some may see cosmopolitan justice as global justice *simpliciter*. When we think about how justice might apply to different people, many would support applying the same general rules for all. If someone were treated differently than others (whether for better or worse), we might raise concerns that an injustice has been done whereby fair treatment means equal treatment. Since cosmopolitanism broadly defends the moral equality of all individuals, the approach has many supporters who see global justice as a project centered on more equal justice for all.

Moreover, there are any number of tragic examples where through an accident of birth someone is living in severe poverty through no fault of their own with all the obstacles to flourishing in life that this brings. Our life chances, opportunities, and longevity can be heavily determined by where we happen to be. For cosmopolitans, morally equally lives are not being lived in morally equal conditions.

Cosmopolitans believe we are all members of an ethically relevant community. The difference with ethical nationalists is that, while the former focus their allegiance to the *national* group, cosmopolitans focus their allegiance to a worldwide community of human beings (Brock 2009:8–9). In the famous words of the ancient Greek philosopher Diogenes the Cynic, "I am a citizen of the world" (Nussbaum 2002:2). In fact, the word "cosmopolitan" comes from the Greek *kosmopolitēs* meaning "citizen of the world."

Cosmopolitans defend different ideas about being a citizen of the world. For example, some distinguish *moral cosmopolitanism* as a normative ideal

---

[1] It is worth noting that liberal nationalists would argue that they take the moral equality of individuals seriously, too, in emphasizing their equal right to self-determination in ethically relevant and justified ways, rather than in a more one-size-fits-all cosmopolitan model (or at least as many liberal nationalists might frame their differences).

versus *institutional cosmopolitanism* focusing on global institutions that provide common standards (Beitz 1999). Others draw a distinction between strong and weak cosmopolitanism. *Strong cosmopolitanism* is the position that all duties to others are general duties to all – and so rejects the use of special associative duties that apply to some, but not others.[2] This is a stronger – and more literal – view of the individual as a citizen of the world and, therefore, a member of a single global community. An illustration of strong cosmopolitanism is the view of Anacharsis Cloots, who advocated the abolition of all states and creation of a single world state inclusive of all humanity in a global "republic of united individuals" (Kleingeld and Brown 2019).

Most cosmopolitans – and the focus of this chapter – are various kinds of so-called *weak cosmopolitans*. This is the view that cosmopolitan justice demands that everyone is at or exceeds a threshold of securing their rights and well-being. It recognizes that some may be higher than others above this threshold. Such a position may appear close to indistinguishable from the liberal nationalists considered in Chapter 4. For example, liberal nationalist David Miller (2007:28) says that if ensuring all individuals are secured justice up to a threshold then "we could safely say that we are all cosmopolitans now." Indeed, we easily find various self-proclaimed cosmopolitans endorsing what we might call a threshold-centered view of justice whereby our primary attention is ensuring all individuals either meet or exceed a given justice threshold (see Nussbaum 2000:70–86).[3]

Both liberal nationalists and cosmopolitans can recognize general and special duties. So, how to differentiate the two? Perhaps the best way is that liberal nationalist put a stronger emphasis on the creation and importance of special associative duties arising in groups. In contrast, weak cosmopolitans – while acknowledging these special duties – emphasize the general duties we have and the consequences that flow from adhering to them.

Cosmopolitan peace

A classic idea in cosmopolitan thought is the view that cosmopolitan justice would lead to world peace. The leading proponent of this view is Immanuel

---

[2] One such argument is that the kinds of things that could be justified as special associative duties are general duties realized differently and shaped by local contexts. In this way, a universalist account might attempt to account for regional variance (see Vernon 2010:20–21).
[3] There are others like Sen (1999) that do not defend a specific threshold, but focus on comparisons of human development toward a ore satisfactory level.

Kant (1957) and his work *Perpetual Peace*.[4] Kant's ethical theory is grounded in universal equality. He defends the idea of a moral law binding on all individuals, as rational human beings. Kant (1996:16) claims that we can determine if an action is right or wrong insofar as it does or not conform with the moral law. The "supreme principle" of the moral law is to "act on a maxim which can also hold as a universal law. – Any maxim that does not so qualify is contrary to morals" (Kant 1996:18). We should reflect on actions and consider if all can do them at the same time. If we can, then it could be a universal law. But if not, then it cannot.

Kant argues that this general formula is helpful for us in determining right from wrong through reason.[5] For example, an individual murdering another is not performing a universal action. It is because the action says one individual should be murdered, but not all – such as not the murderer. In this way, a murderer's action is not universal and contrary to the moral law. Or consider theft. When a thief steals from another, the thief recognizes the value of property ownership in wanting the stolen property as his own possession. But in stealing what is rightfully someone else's, the thief's action denies his victim's right to property while the thief claims his own right to property. Kant's universal moral law can help us understand right and wrong in this way (see Wood 2008). Through applying a universal moral law in different contexts, Kant claims we can ascertain what justice demands in each circumstance.

Similarly, Kant develops a treatise for the perpetual peace among states in a model of universal – and cosmopolitan – justice. He begins with a few preliminary arguments. First, any valid treaty between states must not reserve any tacit option to engage in a future war (Kant 1957:3–4). Treaties are about settling disputes through making an agreement where each party is kept to their word. If a state were only to partly uphold their side of a deal, then they claim to make an agreement in bad faith and render it null and void. Secondly, no state shall come under the dominion of another through inheritance, exchange, purchase or donation (Kant 1957:4–5). This is because the state is sovereign and of its people, not a property to be traded or given away.

Kant's preliminary arguments then become more controversial. Thirdly, he says standing armies should be abolished over time. This is because their continual use is a threatening presence to others (Kant 1957:5–6). Interestingly, Kant (1957:5–6) claims that extreme wealth inequality poses a

---

[4]See *The Global Justice Reader*, chapter 13.

[5]A key criticism of Kant's ethical theory is its reliance – according to these critics – on slavishly following a formula, in what is called the empty formulism objection (see Hegel 1991:162–163; Brooks 2013a:52–61).

similar threat, noting that "[s]uch accumulation of treasure is regarded by other states as a threat of war, and if it were not for the difficulties in learning the amount, it would force the other state to make an early attack." Fourth, and relatedly, Kant (1957:6) says that large debts owed to other states can create friction and poses a "dangerous" risk of conflict to be avoided. Fifth, no state should interfere with the domestic matters of other states in respect of the sovereignty of all states (Kant 1957:7). Sixth, and finally, no state should engage in actions, if at war, that would make a subsequent peace impossible. Kant gives examples like the use of assassins and poisoners. We can easily imagine that if a state fought overly viciously in a conflict that the very difficult path to peace – enormously challenging after any conflict, no matter how short or low intensity the fighting – will be all the worse.

These six preliminary arguments are meant to set the conditions for peace. But this is to be secured through three further "definitive articles." The first is that every state should be republican whereby Kant means the executive and legislative branches are separate (Kant 1957:14–15). The second is that states should form a "league of nations" (Kant 1957:18). The idea is that states could take disputes to a tribunal within their common federation and not need to consider war. Third, and final, Kant claims the citizens of the world should be treated by other states not as enemies, but mere strangers. When we wrong anyone (including a non-citizen) in one state, this impacts on the wider community. Kant says: "a violation of rights in one place is felt throughout the world" (1957:23).

Kant makes several contributions to cosmopolitan thought. First, his argument is that international law based on universal justice is possible without infringing the sovereignty of states. Second, Kant claims a cooperative league of nations is possible and would lead to eternal peace. This view has been taken up and defended by contemporary international relations theorists as the democratic peace theory: democracies do not go to war with each other (Russett 1993). If a state has the right constitution and joins a federation with others, future peace can be secured. Finally, a strong commitment to general duties can support a citizen of the world.

Cosmopolitan patriotism

But can a cosmopolitan citizen *of* the world be a patriot *in* the world? It might appear that we must make a choice. Either we promote our *universal* commitment to all human beings irrespective of national borders – or we attach significance to these boundaries and promote membership with its associative duties as part of a *particular* community. The commitment to cosmopolitanism might clash with any commitment to liberal nationalism. This may seem especially true for Kant, as his cosmopolitan theory sees all human beings, as rational beings, as members of "a single moral community" worldwide (Kleingeld 2000).

To address this issue, Pauline Kleingeld (2000) considers three varieties of patriotism.[6] The first is *civic patriotism* grounded on a republican ideal of free and equal citizens in pursuit of a common political good (Kleingeld 2000:317). It is an inherently political kind of patriotism not dependent on any national or ethnic identity. A second form is *nationalist patriotism* which focuses on the national group that members belong to. Historically, this is the patriotism of the nation-state bound by "native language, cultural community, shared ancestry, common history or other factors, or combinations of these" (Kleingeld 2000:319). The third form is *trait-based patriotism* linked to a love of one's country in relation to its qualities, such as "because it is beautiful, because my personal identity is connected with it in a positive way; because it enables me to live comfortably; because it has laws that promote my well-being; or because I recognize its laws as just or my fellow citizens as virtuous" (Kleingeld 2000:321).

Kleingeld considers each of these three kinds of patriotism to see which might best fit with Kantian cosmopolitanism. Civic nationalism requires for justice that the state has just laws and the power to enforce them to secure individual freedom. It might appear, as Jeremy Waldron (1993), that the pursuit of justice could be considered a moral imperative and, therefore, any Kantian cosmopolitan would have an interest in establishing just political institutions that can settle disputes peacefully and impartially. Kleingeld (2000:327) argues that even if we have a duty to create just states this does not mandate my duty to support a particular state that might be just – nor to owe my compatriots duties that I do not recognize for others.

However, she argues that civic patriotism, if understand in a more cosmopolitan-friendly way, should mean a duty to the "just democratic state" and not a duty toward compatriots *per se* (Kleingeld 2000:332). Our allegiance is to an institution of justice and with an end of justice. Fellow citizens are included within the scope of pursuing this end and so may receive different treatment than non-citizens of other states, but any such activity is not because we aim to treat individuals differently but rather as an unintended by-product of pursuing just institutions that might benefit all. In this way, "Kantian cosmopolitanism and the duty of civic patriotism are compatible" (Kleingeld 2000:335).

---

[6]See *The Global Justice Reader*, chapter 14.

Kleingeld is dismissive of nationalist patriotism's compatibility. While civic patriots focus on love for a just state that all could identify with, nationalist patriots give special attention for one's contingent nationalist affiliation. Kleingeld (2000:336) does not doubt the importance of any community having some sense of affiliation to flourish, but she does doubt that it must be an affiliation based on nationality, if nothing else. Trait-based patriotism is similarly objectionable in that it is based on the particularity of a state which may be contingent and inapplicable for all. Patriotism can be permissible – even compatible – with Kantian cosmopolitanism, but only in its civic conception.

Cosmopolitan justice

One crucially important issue for cosmopolitans is that our life chances can be very different because of an accident of birth. None of us chose where to be born or be raised. Yet, we will have very different opportunities in life to flourish if a part of more affluent countries rather than those in, say, severe poverty. This is an issue for cosmopolitan justice and its universal values because the morally arbitrary feature of where are born can impact some many morally-relevant factors in our lives. If justice is universal, it is not applied the same way for all – and this is a challenge that many cosmopolitans grapple with.

Central to this issue is the lack of equality of opportunity globally. Simon Caney (2001) argues that every liberal society supports the view that every individual should enjoy equality of opportunity with their fellow citizens.[7] However, surprisingly few claim this should be universal for all – both citizens and noncitizens.

Caney (2001:114) argues that everyone "should have the same opportunity to achieve a position, independently of what nation or state or class or religion or ethnic group they belong to." This is not an equality of outcomes. Instead, the aim is procedural – that the same opportunities are available for all to make of them what they wish. No one should be penalized because of the nationality or civic identity they happen to have and unlikely to have chosen. Moreover, global equality of opportunity would especially benefit the least advantage states helping many millions escape severe poverty.

This view may seem a noble, but unrealizable, ideal. For example, we might pose the question of what does it mean to deliver equality of opportunity in

---

[7]See *The Global Justice Reader*, chapter 15.

the same way for every culture? Individuals in different communities may have different conceptions of the good and of how they might wish to fulfil equality of opportunity – and so any common metric might appear elusive. In reply, Caney argues it is a matter of addressing cultural pluralism appropriately in our setting equality out. He notes the example of living standards can be understood in various ways, including in terms of the capabilities approach defended by Amartya Sen and Martha Nussbaum (Caney 2001:121).

A second challenge is to say, following John Rawls, that liberal principles of global justice may not apply to all states, especially non-liberal states (Caney 2001:128).[8] However, in response to Rawls, Caney argues the point is not so much to force liberal principles on non-liberal states, but simply to leave open the equal opportunity, if individuals wished to exercise it. Global equal opportunity requires its being accessible to all and this does not mandate that everyone do so.

One common criticism of cosmopolitan justice is its feasibility. Eradicating poverty or promoting social justice in any society is challenging, but far more difficult in some states than others. This is all the more difficult globally where state-like institutions might not always apply and where enforceability – and, more broadly, deliverability – may not obtain. If any sovereign state might not succeed, what hope the world?

In reply, cosmopolitans might argue that the failure to deliver perfect justice is not a compelling reason to avoid attempting to do as much as we can. For example, we do not say that punishment should be abolished because not every thief or murderer is brought to justice. Nor do we avoid aiming to provide the best education or health care possible even if delivery is uneven or imperfect. Cosmopolitans can say that the world might not be perfectly just, but we should try to make it more so – and such an ideal is a worthy goal even if not fully realizable.

Perhaps there might always be a justice gap between what we seek to achieve and what is delivered. The issue is of degrees and how large a gap we might tolerate. For example, in defending his liberal nationalism, Miller (2007:20) says:

> it is better in the end to be modest and say that the theory of global justice presented here is one made to fit the world in roughly its present condition – a world made up of separate states, each enjoying some degree of autonomy, though markedly unequal in power.

---

[8] See Rawls (1999). This article is included in only the first edition of *The Global Justice Reader*, chapter 11.

The appeal of liberal nationalism is it maps on more closely to the world as we find it. But this is a world of deep structural injustices that defy accept-ability. Perhaps some views of cosmopolitanism raise the bar rather high in what we might seek to achieve. We must separate out what is most compel-ling in theory, but also practice. Which side we weigh up most may influ-ence which conception of justice we wish to defend.

Global philosophy

In defending a view of justice for all, cosmopolitans can sometimes be accused focusing on universal duties to the exclusion of any more par-ticular, special duties. Our world is a place filled with a myriad of differ-ent views of justice and various philosophical traditions. And yet, while the idea of cosmopolitanism can be found in different cultures both Western and Eastern, much of the leading cosmopolitan work appears to operate exclusively in a single philosophical tradition. The issue is whether a philosophy aiming to speak to global concerns in a universal way ought to aspire to becoming a more "global philosophy" (Brooks 2013b:258–259).[9]

Thom Brooks argues that global philosophy is a new horizon for future work in global justice.[10] The idea is that philosophical traditions are typically *bounded*. Each is linked with a sense of belonging and identity, whatever else this might be (Brooks 2013b:256). For example, the liberal tradition is rich and complex ranging from figures like Thomas Hobbes (1996) and John Locke (1988) to T. H. Green (1986) and John Rawls (1971, 1996). Despite their differences, these philosophers work within a common tradition based around the importance of individual rights and consent in ways that others can and do acknowledge as part of a shared tradition.

Such views are considered to be part of a bounded traditions. This is because they operate mostly separate from others. A clear illustration is that strikingly little Western thought about global justice engages in any substantive way with non-Western thought. "We," in the West speak of Hobbes or Rawls and not Han Fei nor Tagore.[11] (The opposite is not true in

---

[9]See *The Global Justice Reader*, chapter 16.

[10]As this book is a survey of leading work in the *Reader*, I will refer to my own work in the third person for consistency and ease of reading.

[11]There are several notable exceptions, especially the work of Martha Nussbaum (2000, 2006).

non-Western thought where greater engagement is more common (see Parekh 2006, Raghuramaraju 2011)).

And yet there is something curious about attempts to tackle global problems from a bounded tradition relying on its own resources in isolation from other traditions. Brooks argues that our global problems are "global" in at least two ways. First, they are global *geographically* in that they are problems found globally. Second, our global problems are global *philosophically* as philosophical issues about justice are an exclusive subject-matter for West nor East. While global justice is about global problems, there is a need for a more globally engaged approach reaching out to other traditions.

Global philosophy is an *unbounded* approach to philosophy, open to engagement with other philosophical tradition. The aim in engaging is to import philosophical resources for utilization within one's chosen approach. Brooks (2013b:258) argues we should be motivated by "the improved ability to address philosophical problem-solving" through redeployment within our tradition of new ideas that might improve our success in offering compelling arguments.

Brooks considers several examples of what this might look like in practice. For instance, contemporary societies are diverse communities where various views of justice may proliferate. One challenge arising from this fact of diverse views about justice is how political stability might be possible over time (see Rawls 1996:3–4). Rawls claims that stability is possible in a particular way. He argues that we must each use what he calls "public reasons" that others might relate to even if they do not share our view of justice. For instance, if we were to make a point based on the importance of, say, human dignity, then this would count because ideas of human dignity can be found in any view of justice. However, if we appealed to the authority of a specific individual or religion, this would not count because such views are not inclusive of any reasonable view of justice. Rawls (1996:131–172) argues we should use these public reasons to create an overlapping consensus. The idea is that reasons that are accessible to all provide a sound foundation for public support for policies that respects the diversity in society.

Rawls's solution to the problem of political stability has its critics. One objection is that any overlapping consensus is too thin and fragile a basis to guarantee future political stability as it goes nowhere near far enough to address the deep differences in society that remain (Wenar 1995). A second objection is Rawls does not have to adopt this model at all to secure stability and so his solution is unnecessary (Barry 1995).

So, how to respond? Brooks says:

> The Indian philosophical tradition offers some possible insights into how this problem might be better addressed. The first insight is to challenge the model of "moral monism" and resistance to cultural pluralism that may be found at the core of much contemporary liberal thought developed from a greater understanding of an "intercultural" view of equality and fairness indebted to Indian philosophical ideas (see Parekh 2006). A further insight might be to claim that political stability might best be secured through a guarantee of a threshold in human capabilities (see Nussbaum 2000). The capabilities approach is to some degree a major achievement of a global philosophy approach with deep roots in multiple traditions, including Aristotelianism and classical Indian philosophy (see Sen 2009). This approach claims that all persons should be guaranteed well-being in terms of the capability to do or be. Political stability might be best secured through the protection of human capabilities

One important point is that some of the concepts or theories in one tradition can crossover into another. For example, there is nothing Western-centric about the concept of well-being and there are conceptions found in non-Western thought as well. The capabilities approaches of Amartya Sen and Martha Nussbaum is a clear example of developing a concept of well-being through drawing on the resources of Western and non-Western traditions that makes a contribution to both.

A second important point is that some of the concepts or theories can be mined from other traditions for redeployment in our own, whatever that might be. Brooks notes that the idea of viewing cultural diversity as a problem for political stability makes culturally specific assumptions. Instead of appealing only to some form of moral monism as a foundation for future peace, we should become open to exploring possibilities of intercultural exchange found in Indian thought where differences are embraced.

In opening up our own philosophical approach to other approaches, the idea is to gather new resources for our approach to better address global challenges. And, of course, philosophical traditions change over time regularly. What is different about global philosophy is it is a more self-conscious cross-tradition approach to doing philosophy. It is not about bringing different traditions together for their own sake nor an attempt to create one – and only one – "true" philosophy that best combines all others (Brooks 2013b:262). Nor is comparative philosophy with its focus on the history of ideas, as important as this work is (see Scharfstein 1998).[12] Instead, global, unbounded philosophy is about addressing challenges that confront us today.

Conclusion

Cosmopolitanism highlights the importance of universal rights and general duties to all. It draws attention to our common humanity – irrespective of our particular nationality – and responsibilities to each other. We are all, in some sense, "a citizen of the world," as Diogenes the Cynic argued. Cosmopolitanism attempts to help us understand our place in it.

We have considered classic work in this area, such as Kant's contributions. His non-consequentialist, universal normative theory grounded in his moral law has wide appeal. Kant's application of this universal theory of justice from the state to the international sphere is, he argues, the possibility of a perpetual peace among states. His views have come to be known as the democratic peace theory and a major contribution in its own right to international political thought.

We then examined the issue of whether cosmopolitanism can be compatible with patriotism. According to Kleingeld, there are different models of patriotism, but only one – civic patriotism – compatible with Kantian-inspired cosmopolitanism. This is because civic patriotism is about our allegiance to justice and pursuit of that end – an ideal that can be true for any state and which does not aim to justify different treatment of individuals based on their nationality thereby prioritizing cosmopolitanism over national identity.

This led us to reflect on cosmopolitan justice. While we might all claim that citizens should enjoy equality of opportunity within a state, surprisingly few claim it should extend across to all states. Caney argues that it should. Our particular nationality should not dictate our life chances, especially where so many live in severe poverty through an accident of birth. While recognizing significant institutional challenges to delivering a global equality of opportunity, Caney claims it is not unfeasible – and the aim of bringing about more justice for more people is a worthy goal.

These discussions of cosmopolitan ideas of justice for all are made within a certain tradition. Brooks argues that global justice's global problems should adopt a more global philosophical approach. The problems faced by

---

[12]For example, see Brown (1953:49–52) comparing Kautilya's *Arthasastra* with Niccolo Machiavelli's *The Prince*.

global justice are shared across philosophical traditions. We should unbound them in seeking to engage with other traditions to develop and reapply new concepts and ideas into our own. This would allow us to make greater use of global philosophical resources to help understand and provide new insights into how global justice – cosmopolitan or not – might be realized.

Discussion questions

1. Can anyone be a "citizen of the world"?
2. How might Kant's cosmopolitanism enable, in his view, perpetual peace?
3. How might cosmopolitanism be compatible with patriotism?
4. What is global equality of opportunity – and is it possible?
5. Is global philosophy the future?

6

Immigration and Citizenship

Introduction

Over the last few decades, there has been increasing attention paid to issues concerning immigration and citizenship.[1] Traditionally, theories of justice focused virtually exclusively on the rights and responsibilities between the state and its citizens. As John Rawls (1996:xlv) says of his own theory, it conceives of us entering at birth and exiting at death.[2] Domestic justice is about a community lived within set borders.

However useful for abstract modelling about justice generally, such a picture does not look like the world we actually live in. Not everyone in any community is a citizen of that state. Our states are sites of citizens living alongside non-citizens. Some of us change our nationality over time and not the same today that we were at birth – or adopt dual nationality. Such issues about how we are raises questions about how we should think about immigration justice and naturalization, i.e. the process of becoming a citizen.[3]

---

[1] A new section was added to *The Global Justice Reader* revised edition to include readings in this area to address this growing interest in the field.

[2] See Rawls (1996:136): "Political society is closed: we come to be within it and we do not, and indeed cannot, enter or leave it voluntarily."

[3] For example, see Brooks (2016b).

Global Justice: An Introduction, First Edition. Thom Brooks.
© 2023 John Wiley & Sons Ltd. Published 2023 by John Wiley & Sons Ltd.

This chapter surveys key work in this area. It begins by examining what control states should exercise over admitting immigrants across its borders – and what, if any, duties there are on both states and immigrant groups. We next focus further on the right to exclude – what it is, how it should work and implications for current practices. Finally, we consider what, if any, threat immigrants pose to national identity as they enter, interact, and become a part of a new community. This raises issues around culture and identity challenging the idea that national identity is fixed or unidimensional. These different areas deepen our understanding of what, if any, right there is for a state to exclude, for the rights and responsibilities between citizens old and new, and the ever-changing nature of national identity.

Immigration as a quasi-contract

Borders are a fact. There is no boundaryless country. We do not live in a world without borders. There are regions where border restrictions might be relaxed. For example, the internal state borders within the European Union, where any of the citizens from the 27 member states have "free movement" within the area. However, like virtually all freedoms, there are restrictions as it is not a right to go wherever one wants to whenever they wish for as long as they like – and many individuals are expelled for breaching the EU's free movement rules each year (see Brooks 2016b:149–180).[4] But the fact of borders is not a normative justification for having them. This normative source must be found.

While none of us chose where to be born, this determines our national citizenship. Our citizenship at birth can have a profound impact on our life chances and opportunities – and perhaps so much so that we may wish, if we can, to relocate by crossing a border and settling somewhere new to build a life within a different country.[5] This raises questions about what rights, if any, we might have to immigrate and what duties, if any, states have, to admit us.

---

[4] I call this the "free movement myth" as EU movement is restricted with enforced removals every year (Brooks 2016b:149–180).

[5] I have this experience first-hand. Originally American and born in New Haven, Connecticut, I later lived in Dublin, Ireland for a couple of years before moving to the United Kingdom where I have lived for over twenty years. I am a dual citizen of the United States and United Kingdom.

One influential view is developed by David Miller (2007:371).[6] He argues there is a "quasi-contractual" relationship between an immigrant group and the citizens of the receiving state. Strictly speaking, it is not a contractual arrangement insofar as the two parties are not in the same position. Miller claims it is "quasi"-contractual as it is about striking a fair bargain, as "immigration typically confers benefits and imposes costs on both parties – the immigrant group and the host society" (Miller 2007:372). Immigrants gain a new home and may acquire new rights of permanent residency and citizenship, while the host society may gain someone who can contribute to the economic and cultural capital of the community.

For Miller, admitting immigrants today poses greater challenges than a century ago. This is because they are to be admitted "as equal citizens, and they have to be admitted on the basis that they will be integrated into the cultural nation" (Miller 2007:376). The challenge is that, for Miller, states used to be able to regard state sovereignty as "a trump card" for restricting entry (Miller 2007:376). However, states no longer have any such unrestrained right to decide who to admit or exclude. Instead, they must justify such decisions in the face of human rights challenges and occasional urgent demands for admittance.

Miller claims that immigrants must have a willingness to accept the responsibilities that come with citizenship. However, he notes that "[t]he difficulty here to specify more precisely what these responsibilities amount to" (Miller 2007:381). Good citizenship should entail respect for the law, a society's liberal principles and, for Miller, a moral obligation to take part in the democratic process, such as through voting. We should also, he says, expect immigrants to play some role in their communities making a contribution. In return, in this quasi-contractual space, the dominant national culture should provide immigrant communities with more resources, if necessary, to support equal citizenship and equal opportunities.

While Miller does not support an assimilation strategy of making immigrant communities morph into the dominant national culture, he does support citizens old and new receiving basic citizenship education. This takes the form of a working knowledge of the national language and a familiarity with that country's history and institutions, such as through a citizenship test (Miller 2007:385). But, to be fair, any such test should not require knowing information inessential for becoming a citizen, such as naming the works of celebrated writers (Miller 2007:385).

---

[6] See *The Global Justice Reader*, chapter 17.

While Miller's discussion is philosophical, it departs in important ways from how immigration works, at least in most Western states. The choice is almost never whether to admit someone at the border as a full citizen with equal rights to everyone in that state or to exclude entirely: there is no such either-or situation. Instead, it is typical that anyone seeking to make their new permanent home in a new country must establish a period of residency first (see Carens 2013:50). For example, in the United Kingdom, an individual must be resident for at least 5 years before being able to apply for permanent settlement – and then wait at least 12 months, if successful in becoming a permanent resident, to obtain citizenship. It is not a question about whether someone appearing for the first time at the border should become an equal citizen today or remain excluded for most countries in fact.

Nor is it clear that a state's right to exclude, at least in principle, is highly constrained. The main group making the kinds of human rights-related claims for immigrating would be typically refugees. However, this group is usually a much smaller immigrant group than individuals immigrating to take up work, study, or reunite with family. Whereas the handling of refugees is mostly constrained by international law, the management of work, study or family visas, the granting of permanent residency and of citizenship are directed primarily by domestic law. This difference is underappreciated in most discussions about immigration and asylum law and policy, as their different sources influence the degree of control a country might apply. A breach of international obligations toward asylum seekers is handled differently than a breach of domestic rules governing long-term residence.

Miller's model of a quasi-contractual relationship makes several assumptions about how good citizenship should operate. Not every state is a democracy with a process to participate in nor liberal principles to defence – and those countries which are democratic do not usually mandate any obligation to take part. Moreover, it is a continuing criticism of citizenship tests that they "never actually test civic competence" which comes from living in the community instead (Carens 2013:59). While no such test should compel an immigrant to adapt specific values, Miller (2016:137) is correct to note the importance of being able to recognize them, such as through a test.

Citizenship tests can play a meaningful role in providing some reassurance to a host country that new citizens can recognize shared values, key political institutions and a familiarity with that country's past. The problem is where the knowledge required of new citizens far exceeds what is known by current citizens. This can undermine the test's purpose for requiring knowledge of new citizens to help integrate with current citizens when the former are held to a different standard. For example, Thom

Brooks (2022a:106) has described the UK's test as "the test for British citizenship that few British citizens can pass." Instead of supporting integration, badly managed tests can undermine it (Brooks 2022b:30–31).

The right to exclude

While states have a right to exclude, as noted by Miller above, and a right which is regularly exercised, it remains unclear how this coercive right should be justified. There will inevitably be at least some unwanted would-be immigrants to exclude – otherwise, there might not be any need for such a right in the first place. So, how might this work?

One important contribution to how we might think about this issue is by Michael Blake (2013).[7] He starts from a position of the state's sovereignty. The state is a territory as well as a legal community with jurisdiction and effective laws within its boundaries. If an immigrant crossed the state's border, the state's inhabitants would have obligations to extend protections to the immigrant's basic rights and, therefore, may have grounds for exclusion. While the right is not absolute, the fact of sovereignty can ground a right to exclude (Blake 2013:104).

Some might argue that the state might have a right to exclude others because of the need to protect a national culture or shared view of the good. Immigrants bring new ideas and potentially different values and cultures that can have an impact. Should states exclude to protect and preserve their culture? Blake rejects this position for three reasons. First, he argues that claims that one culture or shared view should have priority for special protection from other views is objectionable. This is because it "is entirely antithetical to liberal egalitarianism" and so we should not make such claims that some people have greater value than others (Blake 2013:105).

Secondly, Blake claims the argument that there is a particular culture or view of the good that must be protected in *this* state and so our state can exclude unwanted others rests on a mistake. This mistake, for Blake, is that it is "rarely, if ever, true" that any cultural group is found entirely in one state nor any state with only one cultural group within its territory (Blake 2013:105). He argues that we would be wrong to think that our interest in promoting a form of community living gives us any right to that form. Others have rights, too, and our interest is insufficient to justify using coercion to exclude others (see Cole 2001).

---

[7] See *The Global Justice Reader*, chapter 18.

Thirdly, we might argue that citizens of a sovereign state have the right to self-determination – and that this right to determine their future as a group is a right to exclude unwanted non-members from joining their group (see Wellman 2008). Blake (2013:106) rejects this view as giving too much weight to the freedom of associating as a group with the right to exclude unwanted others. This is because immigrants have human rights and these may trump a group's right to exclude them.

In contrast, Blake claims the only way we can justify exclusion is from a jurisdictional standpoint. The sovereign state with an effective government able to exert political and legal control over a territory provides his foundation. Moreover, human beings have rights *qua* being humans. These rights hold universally and may constrain how any state treats any individual. Thus, human rights provide a form of universal protection globally. But human rights protections also require political institutions domestically to defend our human rights and, if necessary, punish their violation (Blake 2013:110–111).

There are a few critical replies that might be offered to these positions. First, we might not be liberal egalitarians. If we are not, then we would reject this view. Perhaps we might support liberal nationalism instead of liberal egalitarianism. If so, we might agree that no such view should be protected – as if we could prevent cultures from changing over time – but that some might be given favored treatment, such as through a national language or shared values. States commonly require newly naturalized citizens to swear oaths of allegiance to their new country, as a citizen, and its values (see Brooks 2016b:46). This could be seen as a prioritization of some values in a new country over those from another, but this seems neither exceptional nor controversial in itself. After all, not every view of the good is pro-democracy or human rights. Requiring new citizens to publicly affirm support for democracy and rights gives greater weight to some views over others – and in a way that political liberalism accepts (Rawls 2001:4–6).

Second, Blake is correct that an immigrant's human rights may serve as trumps to other considerations and so play an important role. However, the overwhelming majority of immigrants to most states (but, admittedly, not all) come to a country through visa pathways facilitating work, study, or family reunion. These areas can and are often restricted through language proficiency requirements, minimum income thresholds, citizenship tests and more. It is common for them to be rights-related exemptions – such as, individuals with learning difficulties are exempt from citizenship tests – but these are more the exception than the rule. The one area where rights play a larger role is with refugees, but these are usually fewer than, say, those immigrating for work: they are distinctly separate categories of migrants both normatively and legally that should not be run together.

To make his argument about how a jurisdictional view can ground a right to exclusion, Blake (2013:112–113) uses a hypothetical thought experiment. Let us turn to this now.

He imagines a French citizen swims to the United States.[8] Blake (2013:112) claims the French swimmer was able to enjoy institutions "legally and morally bound to protect" and fulfil human rights when in France. In leaving France, the swimmer partially abandons its protective institutions. The French swimmer is, however, able to have their universal human rights "protected and fulfilled by the legal institutions of the United States" having arrived on its shore (Blake 2013:113). Moreover, according to Blake (2013:113), Americans acquired "a moral and legal obligation to act in defense" of the French swimmer's human rights which they only obtained after the swimmer came across the border. This happens simply on account of the swimmer's physical presence in the sovereign territory of the United States.

The right to exclude is, for Blake, a right relating to our ability to refuse taking on this additional obligation to protect and fulfil the rights of the immigrant. Blake (2013:120) says:

This general right imposes a duty on would-be immigrants to cite some particular reason why these residents have an obligation to become obligated to these immigrants. In the absence of such a reason, it appears that the state has the right to use coercion to prevent the would-be immigrant from entering into the jurisdiction of the state, since it is the simple fact of presence within that jurisdiction that invokes the obligation to protect the migrant's basic rights.

Individuals do not have a right to immigrate wherever they wish. Would-be immigrants need to have some compelling reason for why others should admit them into their community and provide protection for their rights. If a state is not satisfied by this reason, it can deny entry through coercion if necessary.

It is noteworthy that the discretion for states to accept such reasons is fairly wide. For example, Blake says that, as a Canadian seeking to undertake graduate study across the border in the United States that, he lacked

---

[8]The example might look more plausible, making the same essential points, if the French citizen swam across the English Channel to the United Kingdom which, of course, is at least possible.

any particular right to enter the country. The decision to admit him was purely discretionary and no injustice would transpire if he had been excluded. Arguably, the same might be true if he sought work and was excluded from doing so.

This is in stark contrast to the situation for individuals seeking to leave "underdeveloped and oppressive nations," such as refugees, where the right of an affluent state to exclude them is "rather weak" (Blake 2013:129). This is because the ability for individuals from those states to have their human rights protected might be weak at best. These individuals have an equal right to anyone else in having these rights secured. Affluent states can provide the protections that these individuals lack and generally deserve – and so our right to exclude is weaker than for individuals who have no such needs.

Issues of exclusion can often arise in refugee cases. The Convention relating to the Status of Refugees (1951) defines a refugee as someone who:

> owing to a well-founded fear of being persecuted for reasons of race, religion, nationality, membership of a particular social group or political opinion, is outside the country of his nationality and is unable or, owing to such fear, is unwilling to avail himself of the protection of that country; or who, not having a nationality and being outside the country of his former habitual residence, is unable or, owing to such fear, is unwilling to return to it.

Blake's human rights–centric approach appears well-suited to explain why there are limits on the state's ability to exclude refugees. Refugees have human rights, as set out in the Convention that most countries are signatories to, and those countries are under an obligation to honor their commitment. Refugee rights are not subject to the same discretion that might be applied to other migrants.

But there are some unacknowledged limits here, too. First, while most countries are signatories, not all countries are in support of the Convention. The status of refugees as set out in the Convention is, at least in practice, dependent on their legal recognition. We might all be readily persuaded – as most of the world's government are – that refugees have rights and that these flow from the convention. We may claim that every country should accept this view of rights, but this argument needs to be made.

One issue is that some of the non-signatories are "underdeveloped and oppressive nations" in the sense Blake (2013:129) notes. Let us call them *underdeveloped states* for short. So, the issue is if *every* state ought to accept refugees from an underdeveloped state because their rights are insufficiently protected, what about underdeveloped states themselves? Arguably, there may be some duty to provide such protections and they are in an unjustifiable state until this is enabled. Yet, underdeveloped states play a major role in accepting large numbers of refugees from other underdeveloped states. We might want to claim that they should do so and that perhaps their rights, in finding asylum or refuge, are better protected than in their home country. But, if so, it could be argued the right to exclude those in need is weak for both developed or underdeveloped states.

Secondly, Blake's account overlooks the importance of other issues, such as national security. Potential immigrants who pose a threat to national security of a host country, if admitted, are clearly grounds for exclusion. Even advocates of more open borders, such as Joseph Carens (2013:175, see 225–254), describes such examples as "nothing intrinsically problematic." The main concern is where such grounds for exclusion are abused, not that they are used.

Finally, countries might be justified in admitting immigrants who wish to resettle in their territory. But what of the impact on the communities they leave behind? This is the issue of *brain drain* (Brock 2021:163–178). For example, refugees are individuals able to find asylum. They are the individuals who were able to leave their home country and seek safety elsewhere. It is not uncommon to find doctors, teachers, architects, scientists, technology experts, and other highly skilled individuals correctly recognized as refugees fleeing persecution.

Brain drain is where high skilled workers leave to find opportunities elsewhere. When we accept these individuals as either worders or refugees in affluent countries, they contribute to our community with their skills. Their former country must rebuild and develop without them. This raises the particular problem of affluent states failing to train enough of their own citizens in order to hire noncitizens trained abroad at lower salaries than would be paid to citizens. The state incurs significant costs in training its citizens to become doctors and scientists. It is an investment in that country's future. So, if these highly qualified and expensively trained citizens leave before this investment is returned through contributing in skilled employment, the state makes a loss on the talent it invests in.

Blake (2017) argues that there can be a right of states to restrict emigration. He claims that emigration can be restricted as an emergency response to unfavorable circumstances. An important qualification is that the response is an "emergency" which denotes it is meant temporarily only. This is because, for Blake, any such restriction is a wrong, albeit a permissible wrong, to address some crucial problem urgently, such as a lack of doctors to adequately run a health service in short term.

These different scenarios – of immigrating swimmers and would-be emigrant doctors – usefully point out how restrictions can run both ways. There may be a right to prevent emigration and a right to prevent immigration. The rights of individuals and of groups to self-determine might each have relevance, but how they relate may differ depending on circumstances.

Immigration and national identity

Our common citizenship is what unifies us in a divided world (see Miller 2000:41). This unity of a community based around a shared history or values could, it might be argued, be put under threat from immigration. Immigrants may arrive with different values, languages, or religions that could be seen to dilute whatever commonality exists within the group as a whole. This raises the question of what, if anything, should a country be able to do about preserving its current national identity in light of future immigration?

Samuel Scheffler (2007:94) says:

> The features and practices that define the host nation's distinctive identity – the very features that give its non-immigrant citizens the sense of belonging to a single people – are experienced by immigrants as unfamiliar at best, and alienating or oppressive at worst. All too often, the symbols of inclusion and commonality are thus transformed into emblems of exclusion and discord. Once this happens, a country has in theory only two choices. It can resort to a kind of cultural apartheid, refusing to grant equal recognition or status to the traditions and practices of the newcomers, and enforcing as best it can the symbols of the old identity. Or it can abandon the old identity and reconceive itself as a multicultural society with a new, pluralistic identity.[9]

Scheffler argues that the first choice could seem preferable. A country might be thought to have some right to the preservation of its culture and identity, so long as this is not intrinsically unjust or oppressive. Since large scale immigration could threaten change, the state might legitimately limit the numbers of immigrants accepted.

Scheffler fleshes out his position with an appeal to the true life story of his father. He was sent from what is now Poland on his own to a family in Glasgow around 1911 before travelling onwards to New York City a few

---

[9] See *The Global Justice Reader*, chapter 19.

years later. On arrival into the United States, Scheffler's grandfather was noted in the immigration database as a "Hebrew" with Austrian nationality (Scheffler 2007:96).

Scheffler asks the question – so what is his father's culture? It is claimed he could hardly count himself Polish as Poland was not yet a state when he left as a teenager nor was he of Polish stock. Nor was his culture of the Hapsburg Empire of his original citizenship. While he took his religion seriously, Scheffler (2007:97) notes that like most religions there are many different "versions and variants" making talk of any single "Jewish 'culture'" elusive.

This story helps establish several key points. The first is that we should not assume that we can identify a single culture to which every immigrant belongs (Scheffler 2007:99). Our culture, if any, need not – and may not – be fixed in any determinable way. Instead, it is fluid and it may keep changing over a life. Scheffler notes that individuals pick out different aspects of their identities as defining, whether it is religion, their occupation, trade union activity, race, gender, or sexual orientation. Some are more attentive to these aspects than others. (Despite having lived abroad for over a decade, I did not identify myself as an immigrant for several years, for example, until it was time to apply for permanent residency and pass a British citizenship test in 2009.) Scheffler claims that we may each have changing identities or multiple identities that change over a life. We should not expect everyone to have a fixed identity based around a single source of identity (Scheffler 2007:101).

The second key point is immigrants immigrate for a variety of different reasons, but the one thing they have in common is that immigration is change. As Scheffler (2007:102) notes, "that's the point of it. It changes the immigrants and it changes the host country." Immigrants change as they adapt to new surroundings, gain fluency in new accents and languages, befriend new people, engage with new institutions and experience new ideas and customs. Scheffler (2007:103) notes the "'national culture' will change," too. New arrivals bring new ideas that help contribute and shape local culture. To take a famous example, chicken curry is one of the most popular dishes in Britain made popular through the country's heritage as a former Empire whose "jewel in the crown" was India.[10] Britain's heritage helps define contemporary Britishness; our collective past informs our collective present (Brooks 2016b).

---

[10] See BBC, "Why Was India so valuable to the British Empire?" (9 November 2012), url: https://www.bbc.co.uk/programmes/p0167gq4.

But what if we wanted to close the borders allowing no foreigners to settle in our country? Scheffler considers this hypothetical. He notes that it is impossible to imagine a national culture remaining unchanged decades into the future – even if the only future citizens are our offspring. Scheffler (2007:104) says:

> To think that this is either possible or desirable is to imagine nothing at all happening in or to the country in the intervening period: no new ideas, no new challenges, no new discoveries or inventions, no advances in science or medicine or technology, no new works of literature or art or music, no new heroes or villains, no changes in fashion or style or enter-tainment, no new achievements, no new successes, no new failures . . . it cannot mean this. Cultures survive only by changing, by accumulating and interpreting and producing new ideas and experiences. There is no other way.

Essential to this point is the view that immigration changes the culture of the immigrant, but also of the host country. There is no option of keeping any country's national identity set in stone for eternity. As its people and their circumstances change, their national identity evolves – whether or not immigration is heavily restricted.

Scheffler (2007:112) argues that we should adopt a kind of "Heraclitean pluralism." Famously, the ancient Greek philosopher Heraclitus claimed all things are constantly changing. For example, in Heraclitus' view, we "could not step into the same river twice" as the river is ever-changing (Plato 1997:120).[11] Likewise, for Scheffler, our national identities shape and shift over time. There is no possibility of preserving unaltered either the national culture of the host country nor the imported culture of immigrations – as each impacts the other. We should accept "a pluralist framework" in thinking about the relation of national identity and immigration (Scheffler 2007:109).

We might think that this would lead to a multiculturalist position to engage with this pluralism. However, Scheffler (2007:117–118) opposes cultural rights and multiculturalism claiming they "add little that is useful" and provide "an invitation to mischief" in encouraging us to think in "strong-preservationist terms." This appears based on the view that multiculturalism is divisive in nature refocusing our attention more on our differences than our commonalities.

---

[11] This is from Plato's *The Cratylus* at 402a.

Moreover, Scheffler (2007:119) rejects the idea that cultural identity can generate normative justification – in contrast to moral, religious, and philosophical convictions which, in his view, can. This is not an issue about which identity is preferred by the individual. Scheffler is careful to acknowledge that our cultural identity can matter to us as much as moral, religious, or philosophical identities. Furthermore, cultural identity is thought incompatible with liberal thought – and too fluid a notion to warrant formal protection even if it was not. For these reasons, he admits general skepticism about the moral significance of our attachments and group affiliations (Scheffler 2007:123).

Scheffler's rejection of a multiculturalist approach, however, is not convincing. It is unclear why multiculturalism must necessarily be divisive and contrary to political harmony – and unlike any other moral, religious, or philosophical conviction. For example, multicultural approaches to national identity, such as Bhikhu Parekh's (2006), champions prohibiting discrimination, promoting racial equality and supports educating school children about different cultural traditions should, instead, foster a more deeply engaged and tolerant society. In contrast, we might say it is precisely in *not* prohibiting discrimination, *not* promoting racial equality and failing to teach children about difference that can breed intolerance, poisonous to any sense of community (Uberoi 2018).

Finally, our cultures and national identities are not the only identities in flux. So, too, our understandings of moral, religious, and philosophical convictions. Each of these is shaped by their time and circumstances in a variety of ways – similarly to cultural change. If we seek a Heraclitean pluralism, multiculturalism remains an option.

Conclusion

Ours is a world of borders – where individuals have crossed these borders since they were established. This raises a number of questions about the rights of individuals to immigrate, the rights of countries to restrict emigration and immigration, the requirements for becoming a permanent member and citizen, and the impact of immigrants on national identity.

As our world becomes ever more interconnected, these issues inevitably arise. They challenge our traditional thinking about justice for citizens within a shared state to consider the admittance of new members and conditions for equal citizenship. For example, we might think that prospective immigration enter into a quasi-contractual relationship with the members of their new country. There are rights and responsibilities that work both ways. Immigrants gain benefits from membership as does their host country. But there may be conditions placed on prospective immigrants regarding language proficiency or other requirements to have the opportunity for full membership as a citizen. Likewise, the state has various duties to prospective members to support and accommodate them within their new home.

At the same time, every country has – and exercises – its right to exclude others. Yet, it is not always clear how such a right might work. We have considered one influential answer from Blake, who claims the state does have a right to exclude but it is constrained – and may be trumped – by rights-relevant demands, such as of asylum seekers to refugee status. Furthermore, the original home country can exercise a right to prevent emigration, such as in temporary, emergency conditions. States can both include as well as exclude through controls on immigration and emigration.

Of course, new immigrants might bring a different cultural perspective to their new host country. Some might be concerned about the impact of these new ideas on existing national identity seeking to protect it from change by immigration. As we have seen, national identity is an ever-changing concept that even a total ban on immigration would fail to prevent. The issue is how to think about changing national identities that unite communities. The readings discussed in this chapter help us make some progress towards this.

Discussion questions

1. Is there a contractual relationship between immigrants and their new country?
2. When might a state be justified in excluding immigrants?
3. Does anyone have a right to immigrate or become a citizen of whatever country they choose?
4. Why might brain drain be a problem and should there by any right of a state to prevent emigration to deal with it?
5. Does immigration strengthen or threaten a country's national identity?

7

Global Poverty

Introduction

When we think about global *justice*, we most often talk about global *poverty*. Global distributive justice is an area receiving more attention from scholars and policymakers than any other.[1] It is easy to see why. Consider the following facts. Nearly half of the world's population – a total of 3.4 billion people – struggle to meet basic needs living on less than US$5.50 a day. According to the World Bank (2018), about one-third of these live in extreme poverty surviving on less than US$1.90 daily – this is an annual income of US$693.50.

This chapter surveys leading contributions to how we might think about what to do about this urgent problem. We consider the positive and negative duties as well as remedial responsibilities to provide assistance. So, what should this look like? Should support be mostly in terms of money and funding – or in terms of capabilities and freedom?

Severe poverty is not a hypothetical puzzle, but a widescale human tragedy requiring urgent intervention. What we can do matters. Therefore, we next consider the moral relevance of practices in thinking

---

[1] In 2008, I described this area as *international* distributive justice. See the first edition of *The Global Justice Reader*, part VII. The revised edition re-titles this simply as "Global Poverty."

Global Justice: An Introduction, First Edition. Thom Brooks.
© 2023 John Wiley & Sons Ltd. Published 2023 by John Wiley & Sons Ltd.

about this issue. This bears on the historical legacy of practices, such as colonialism, that will be examined as well and the concept of rectificatory justice.

What to do about severe poverty in the world is one of the biggest challenges for global justice theorists. The leading ideas and philosophers below contribute enormously to how we might think about this challenge – and how it might be best addressed.

Positive duties

Let us begin considering perhaps the most famous thought experiment in the global justice literature:

> if I am walking past a shallow pond and see a child drowning in it, I ought to wade in and pull the child out. This will mean getting my clothes muddy but this is insignificant, while the death of the child would presumably be a very bad thing. (Singer 1972:231)[2]

Peter Singer's hypothetical example of the *drowning child* contains a lot of argument and complexity in a seductively succinct way which has been a focal point for discussions since its publication in 1972.

Imagine carefully this scene. You are walking along a pond. You notice there is a child drowning and urgently needs help. One assumption is that there is no one else who might act or rescue the child more quickly. Note that we do not know how or why the child came to be in the pond either. All we know is that the child requires urgent help or they will drown.

The pond is described as shallow. So, presumably, it is deep enough to be over the child's head but shallow enough to pose no risk of drowning or life risking behavior for us in entering the water and saving the child. Singer notes that while our clothes would become muddy if wading through the pond towards the child this is an insignificant problem for us in acting in comparison to the significant problem for the child's death if we did not act.

This notion of significance refers to moral significance, or what I would call the relevant *moral cost*. Singer (1972:231) claims "if it is in our power to prevent something bad from happening without thereby sacrificing anything of comparable *moral* importance, we ought, morally,

---

[2] See *The Global Justice Reader*, chapter 20.

to do it."[3] We weigh the moral cost of our action *to us* against the moral cost of inaction *to others*. Singer argues that if the moral cost in taking action to us is less than the moral cost in not taking action to others, then we should do it.

Muddying our clothes – even if wearing an expensive tuxedo that becomes ruined – to save another's life might always be morally required on Singer's view. This is because we are not weighing the *monetary* cost of our action, but its *moral* cost. The moral value of dirtying our clothes falls short of the moral value of a child's young life.

But suppose instead that we pass by the pond because we are being pursued by an assassin attempting to kill us. We see the drowning child as we approach the water's edge. Let us assume that if we diverted ourselves from running away from the assassin to save the child that the assassin would instead catch up and kill us. In this hypothetical example of the *drowning child and the assassin*, the moral cost to us would be very high – our death – and not less than the moral cost to the child – their death – in our inaction. We need not save the child out of a positive duty in such a case.

Singer defends the idea of a *positive duty*. The claim is that, if we can help, we should help. It does not matter how the child came into distress. It does not matter if it was only you or me that happened to walk down a path alongside the pond that day – whoever is able to provide assistance to others, where the moral cost to us in acting is less than the moral cost to others in our inaction, has a duty to provide assistance to others.

Singer's example of the drowning child is supposed to show us that most, if not all, of us in affluent countries have a positive duty to provide support to those in severe poverty. It does not matter whether the urgent plight of others was a result of our choices or of our government's choices. Nor does it matter if we lack any connection to those in need beyond sharing a common humanity. Like the stranger child in a pond, we should do what we can if we can, regardless of other factors. Our providing assistance is not an act of *charity*, but an act of *duty* – our positive duty to act.

The example is also meant to show that distance or proximity is irrelevant from what Singer (1972:231) calls "the moral point of view." Consider the example of the *distant drowning child*. Suppose I am an astronaut exploring the moon in outer space. NASA contacts me to say that there is a drowning child. As it happens, I can simply press a button inside my rocket sat on the moon and, if I do so, a dam will open that will lower the pond water so the child will be saved and able to walk to dry land unscathed. The moral cost to me in pausing my space

---

[3] Emphasis added.

exploration is less than the moral cost to the child and their death in my not acting. The fact that I am distant – or even not on the Earth – is irrelevant when weighing the relevant moral costs.

There is also a second assumption. The act of global justice is performed by the adult able to wade through the water and received by the child unable to stay afloat. This provides a dichotomy of affluent states as the active actors and those in severe poverty as the passive patients – that might appear to some as paternalistic in a literal, and perhaps problematic, sense.

Of course, Singer's example is succinct and meant only to establish that there is a positive duty to act in similar cases and how the weighting of moral costs should work. Nonetheless, we might raise the issue of the agency of the saved – and not only the saving. In a scenario as described, the child would likely welcome any assistance. But where there is a choice or other factors at play, they might wish another who might act to do so – or support in creating their own floatation device so they might rescue themselves with the minimally required intervention of others to make that possible.

Negative duties

Let us consider a different version of the drowning child example:

> You are walking alongside a pond. You watch an assassin throw someone in a pond. This someone will drown if not saved. Both the assassin and you could save them from drowning.

From the standpoint of Singer's defense of positive duty, *both* the assassin *and* you have a positive duty to act. Moreover, the weight of this duty is the same. Your ability to save the drowning person is equal to the assassin's. It does not matter who, if anyone, was responsible for the need of urgent rescue. What does matter is that someone – namely, both of you – could save the person at no greater cost to yourselves.

While we might remain convinced there is a positive duty to act, we might still insist that the assassin has a stronger duty to rescue. This is not because he can save the person more quickly, but because the assassin bears responsibility for the need of rescue. When someone has some responsibility connected to why another requires rescue, this someone has a *negative duty* to act. We have a negative duty in relation to our responsibility.

Our negative duty is more stringent than a positive duty. Consider the following example of *two drowning persons*. Suppose you are walking alongside a pond and accidentally bump into someone who falls into the water. At that moment, a second person completely oblivious to what just happened slips along the water's edge and falls into the pond. Both persons will drown unless saved. You are only able to save one. Both are complete strangers to you. Whom do you save?

In terms of positive duties, we have a positive duty to both that is equal. We are able to save both, say, at no greater moral cost in acting than the cost to them if we walked away. Positive duties would have us flip a coin.

But in terms of *negative duties*, we were responsible for one of the two falling in. There are two ways we might think about it. The first is we have a positive duty to both, but an additional negative duty to one. If we add up our duties to each, then we would choose to save the individual we had responsibility for bumping into the pond. The second way is to say that our negative duties, as linked to our responsibilities, have greater relative weight than our positive duties. In weighing up our positive duty to one, but a negative duty to the other, we should choose to prioritize our negative duty when we must make this otherwise very difficult choice. The evidence is grounded in our intuitions about justice when we reflect on what makes most compelling sense.

The idea of negative duties and their relevance was popularized by Thomas Pogge (2001).[4] The general position is that we have a negative duty to put right what we have made wrong. When we are responsible for causing harm or serious risk of harm to others, we have a duty to rectify in ending our harm or risk of harm and repairing any damage caused.

Pogge develops this argument into the claim that citizens of affluent countries owe a negative duty to those living in severe poverty. The argument might be summarized as follows:

1. Citizens in affluent countries are predominantly democratic societies.
2. Citizens elect their political leaders who decide directly, or choose representatives on their behalf indirectly, matters relating to an international global order.
3. The international global order includes institutions like the IMF and World Bank.
4. This global order knowingly, foreseeably, and avoidably perpetuates a system that maintains severe poverty because its monetary agreements favor affluent states at the expense of developing countries and

---

[4]This article is included in only the first edition of *The Global Justice Reader*, chapter 22. It is reprinted in Pogge (2002).

there are protectionist exemptions favoring affluent states as well (see Pogge 2002:18–19).[5]

Pogge's conclusion is that citizens of affluent countries have a negative duty to those in severe poverty because the international global order that is controlled by their democratic states maintains a global system that perpetuates conditions allowing for the continuation of severe poverty (Pogge 2002:129–30).[6] If our leaders had chosen to operate the global order differently so it did not have that effect, then we might not have a negative. But until this happens, we do. Pogge (2010:2) says: "World poverty is actively perpetuated by our governments and officials, and knowingly so. We citizens, too, have enough information to know what is going on, or at least to find out easily, if we care." We are all implicated in the continuation of severe poverty and must act to end this harm to others – and, to be clear, Pogge (2007) sees the imposition of denying basic needs through severe poverty as a human rights violation.

One criticism of the argument is not all affluent countries in the world are democratic – and so the shared responsibility of affluent democratic states for the negative effects from any international global order is only partial. In reply, Pogge rejects this criticism arguing that countries are effectively contributing to a joint enterprise where all who participate bear responsibility

---

[5] In seminar discussions, my students have found it relatively unclear how the steps taken from the democratic citizen through to their state onto global institutions and their impact on those in severe poverty make the citizens responsible where their leaders may make choices (and appoint individuals who make choices) far removed from their ballot on election day. A common concern raised is that with each step of the argument, as we move further away from the direct activity of citizens as agents, it might be said that the responsibility of citizens weakens. Or others argue that citizens vote for candidates mostly, if not exclusively, on the back of local issues – not everyone is a global justice theory prioritizing global justice issues. It is not they who bear the brunt of decisions made by others – who may have been elected on the back of domestic policies, not foreign policy proposals – but the elected leaders and their representatives who act on the behalf of others. There is much to be said for and against each view that would take another chapter (or two) to handle adequately. But for the purposes of critically surveying the main ideas, these issues merit reflecting on in future seminars. Our choices, whatever they are, may have consequences. Similarly, our political leaders and their representative public officials, whoever they are, have significant responsibilities. Both have relevance in thinking through what, if any, negative duties may be held, who has a negative duty to act and their relative weight (see Armstrong 2012:28–30).

[6] See Brooks (2007:526–527).

for the wrongs that flow from their actions in full. In response, it could be argued that we distinguish between, for example, the main offender and their accomplices who aid and abet their crimes. All contribute to wrongs and deserve punishment, but this punishment is proportionate to their contribution – and not equally shared by defaulters (Brooks 2020e).

A second criticism of the argument is that citizens in affluent democratic states that take every action possible to elect political leaders and support public policies that do not support an international global order perpetuating severe poverty do *not* appear to share in any collective negative duty. If I do not give neither active nor tacit consent to my state's engagement in contributing to a global harm and if I do everything possible to prevent it, then it is not at all clear why I should be held to contribute to my state's wrongful decision-making that I have done so much to oppose and correct. In democracies, it is true that citizens should accept the outcome of free and fair elections. But recognizing procedural outcomes is not the same as endorsing political decisions: election victories create mandates from the size of the support. I can recognize that a political candidate has received a mandate to serve as President or Prime Minister without contributing myself to that mandate in putting my support elsewhere – and, if I do so, it is unclear why, in giving no support to this mandate, I might be held normatively responsible for whatever is done with this mandate that others, not me, supported.

In reply, it might be said that, if I did not support the mandate of an elected official who went on to support an international global order that continued to engender severe poverty, I might still have a duty to support ending severe poverty. However, instead of a negative duty to correct a wrong for which we are responsible for contributing toward, we might have a positive duty to act if we can.

Pogge proposes that we can act to fulfil our negative duty through paying a *Global Resources Dividend*. This is effectively a tax priced at an extra US$2 per barrel of oil. The idea is that affluent countries are the biggest users of oil. This use contributes to climate change's harmful effects that have a disproportionately negative effect on the developing world, including areas of severe poverty. A Global Resources Divided is a way of raising resources from affluent countries to contribute to poverty alleviation and help correct the continuing problems in the international global order (Pogge 2001:66–71).

One issue that might be raised with this proposal is the following. It is a plan for raising resources from now on for alleviating existing poverty. At least hypothetically, affluent states might choose to start switching off from fossil fuels to alternative green energy. While having had a negative duty, they might avoid paying into the Global Resources Dividend.

Metaphorically speaking, the guilty would not be punished for their wrongs. In reply, Pogge (2001:72) says that even if his proposal is not realistic, there remains an important wrong to address and we have a negative duty to act. But if this proposal will not fully address the problem, it can only be a partial solution – and we must do more to reflect on how any negative duties might be fulfilled through some alternative measure (see Cohen 2010). As Pogge (2007:4) says: "the real task is to end severe poverty on this planet." We can agree with this aim even if we remain unconvinced about how to determine negative duties and a workable plan to fulfil them.

Remedial responsibility

We have considered positive and negative duties. Some might say that these alone are insufficient for addressing severe poverty. One reason might be that we lack the resources to go as far as needed in acting on any positive duty toward others without doing ourselves harm. A second reason could be that other states bear a negative duty, and not ours, and so the problem remains until this is resolved.

Nevertheless, justice demands that some duty of assistance is acted upon those in urgent need for their survival (see Rawls 1999:118).[7] It is undoubtedly clear that something must be done even if, thus far, we may remain unclear about what is to be done.

In an important contribution to this issue, David Miller argues that we must go beyond the positive or negative duties debate. This is important as some cases of severe deprivation might not be caused directly by the actions of other states, such as damage from a tsunami, and no clearly discernible negative duty arising. Miller (2001:453) says:

> Nearly all of us believe that this is a situation that demands a remedy: someone should provide the resources to end the suffering and deprivation. The problem does not here, but in deciding which particular agent or agents should put the bad situation right. Very often there are many agents who could act in this way. The issue is how to identify one particular agent, or group of agents, as having a particular responsibility to remedy the situation. For unless we do this, there is a danger that the suffering or deprivation will continue unabated, even though everyone

---

[7]This article is included in only the first edition of *The Global Justice Reader*, chapter 11.

agrees that it is morally intolerable, because no-one is willing to accept the responsibility to step in and relieve it.[8]

Miller (2001:454) calls this the problem of *remedial responsibility*, i.e., a responsibility to provide remedy to others. He addresses this problem by clarifying, first, the relevant kinds of agents of global justice and, second, the connections through which we may assign remedial responsibilities to these agents.

Whereas Singer and Pogge start from examples relating to individual responsibility, Miller begins noting the importance of national groups.[9] As we have seen in Chapter 4, Miller (1995:49–80) defends the normative significance of our national group membership and the associative duties it creates.[10] He defines his liberal nationalism as about "a body of people who share a common identity, involving cultural values, attachment to a territory, and so forth, and who aspire to institutions of political self-determination which they may or may not actually enjoy" (Miller 2008:143).

Miller argues that remedial responsibility is about selecting the most appropriate nations, as agents of global justice, to provide remedy to those in severe poverty. An illustration may help clarify the relevance of having associative duties. Consider the following. Imagine you are walking past a pond when you notice two children drowning. You only have time to save one of them. The child on your left is a complete stranger with no known connection to you. The child on the right is your offspring. If our personal attachments did not matter, we might flip a coin and randomly pick which child to rescue.

However, Miller's compelling point is our attachments have ethical significance. In this situation of *our drowning child*, we would expect any parent in this tragic circumstance to save their child. This is no injustice to the unsaved child. It is not a matter of failing to respect our general duty to rescue, but recognizing our additional associative duty – above and beyond our general duty to save both children – that makes a difference and helps us make a choice.

---

[8] See *The Global Justice Reader*, chapter 21.

[9] As a reminder, Singer's argument for positive duties begins with a hypothetical example of passing a pond where there is a drowning child. Pogge's argument for negative duties begins with our individual responsibility, as citizens of an affluent democratic state, for the leaders and their representatives who make decisions on our behalf that maintain severe poverty. Miller will begin by talking about the importance of nations.

[10] This chapter is included in only the first edition of *The Global Justice Reader*, chapter 14.

Let us modify the example. Now suppose you are walking past a pond noticing there are two children who require rescue. The child on your left lacks any known connection to you. The child on the right is known to you and they are from your neighborhood and of your national group. While the attachment may be weaker than with one's child, we have general duties to both children but, again, we have an additional associative duty to those we recognize as our conationals. We might expect anyone in this awful situation to rescue those with whom there is a recognized attachment. Our associative duties help us choose. And no wrong is done by us to the second child we cannot also save.

Miller claims our group membership as a nation has normative significance and can make a difference for how we should act. However, as Thom Brooks (2014b) has argued, our national groups are not the only such groups that can have this significance – and can serve as additional agents of global justice to assign remedial responsibilities to.[11] Miller says national group membership is valuable because the shared identity is intrinsically valuable, it is integral to our relationship and honoring the normative significance of our group's membership does not compel us to deny what we may owe others.

Brooks claims national groups are not unique in this respect as organized religious groups could also fit this model. Using the example of the Catholic Church, Brooks notes that membership can fulfil all the same aspects of national group identity. The importance of this finding is that when we consider who should provide rescue to those in need our focus should be on all agents of global justice who might fulfil remedial responsibilities whether a nation or nonnational group. Indeed, because of colonial history or other factors, there may be times where it may be preferable for a nonnational group to provide remedy than a nation (Brooks 2014b).

Now that we have made clear the kinds of groups – both nations and non-national groups – that could be agents of global justice, we next turn to the issue of how we might assign remedial responsibilities to any such agent. Miller argues for his *connection theory* of remedial responsibility. He claims: "The basic idea here is that A should be considered remedially responsible for P's condition when he is linked to P in one or more ways" (Miller 2007:99). Miller lists the following factors that we are to consider and the questions each addresses:

1. *Causal responsibility*: was a nation causally responsible for bringing about suffering and deprivation elsewhere? (Miller 2007:101–102).

---

[11] See *The Global Justice Reader*, chapter 22.

2. *Moral responsibility*: was a nation morally responsible for bringing about suffering and deprivation elsewhere? (Miller 2007:100).
3. *Capacity*: does a nation have the capacity to provide a remedy? (Miller 2007:103–104).
4. *Community*: is a nation amongst any particular community shared with a nation suffering deprivation whether it be "ties of family or friendship, collegiality, religion, nationality, and so forth"? (Miller 2007:104).
5. *Outcome responsibility*: is the suffering and deprivation faced elsewhere a side effect of any nation's activities? (Miller 2007:100–101).
6. *Benefit*: did a nation benefit from the suffering and deprivation elsewhere even if the former played no causal role in the latter? (Miller 2007:102–103).

Miller argues we are to consider these factors together in relation to each relevant (national or nonnational) group to determine how we should distribute their relevant remedial responsibilities. In so doing, we are to "rely on our intuitions about the relative importance of different sources of connection" (Miller 2007:107).

Formally, Miller claims that each connection is no more important than another. Each should be considered equally without any priority between them. He says:

> We might think, therefore, that some forms of connection should always be given priority over others; I shall argue, however, against this. The point to bear in mind is that the weight of justification is borne by the pressing need to relieve P, and the necessity of identifying a particular agent as having the obligation to provide the relief. The fact that some of the links appear morally flimsy when taken by themselves matters less when this point is grasped. (Miller 2007:99–100)

This may, in fact, make our task all the more challenging. If there is no way of ranking the six different kinds of connections, it is unclear how we might decide how to assign remedial responsibilities.

Let us consider an example. Suppose one national group has *moral responsibility* for the suffering elsewhere, perhaps on account of having briefly militarily attacked it without provocation, but no other connection. A second national group is part of the same *community* as the nation that was attacked, as they share a common language, but no other connection either. On an intuitive level, it would seem clear that most of us would say that the nation with a moral responsibility for causing suffering and deprivation elsewhere would have a much stronger remedial responsibility than another nation that so happens to also speak the same language as the group suffering deprivation. These connections might be formally equal, but we would not weigh them equally. Miller (2007:107) appears to acknowledge this issue when he says that "I assume … that negative duties weigh more heavily than positive ones." Nonetheless, his view remains that none have any priority over the others and each is to be considered on their equal merits.

Thom Brooks (2002a, 2011) claims that Miller's connections are not all equal. This can be made plain in an example. Consider which nation to assign a responsibility to remedy where each has only the following single connections:

1. Nation A is causally responsible for deprivation in Nation X.
2. Nation B is morally responsible for deprivation in Nation X.
3. Nation C has the capacity to provide a remedy to Nation X.
4. Nation D shares a national religion with Nation X.
5. Nation E is outcome responsible for deprivation in Nation X.
6. Nation F benefited from the deprivation in Nation X.

Strictly speaking, only option 3 (Nation C) could be assigned a remedial responsibility. This is because only a nation with the capacity to provide a remedy can deliver on its remedial responsibilities. No matter how strong the other nations' connections might be, they lack the capacity to remedy and so cannot be assigned remedial responsibilities.

This example highlights a two-step process. We first determine which relevant groups have the capacity to deliver remedies. We next weigh the strength of any other connections – as these only become relevant for those groups that have capacity. While the six connections are presented as equally meritorious, they clearly fall into this two-step process.

This seems implicitly acknowledged, if not formally accepted, within Miller's account. Speaking of more hypothetical examples of drowning individuals, he says:

> Carelessly pushing someone into a river is blameworthy, but not as bad as pushing them deliberately. Are we to say that a careless pusher who is also a weak swimmer should be held responsible for the rescue in prefer-ence to the lifeguard who make the rescue easily and safely? *Getting P out of the river seems more important here than enforcing the moral responsibility of the pusher.* (Miller 2007:105)[12]

---

[12] Emphasis is added.

We should weigh up all connections generally, but what matters is the outcome that a remedy is provided – and, in the above example, that P is rescued from the river. The capacity of the lifeguard to rescue trumps connections like causal or moral responsibility. It must be emphasized that it is no criticism of the connection theory – as a theory of global distributive justice – to claim it operates in a two-step process. While different from how it is originally presented, Miller's theory does provide an original way of thinking about how remedial responsibilities can be assigned here and now to aid those requiring urgent rescue.

However, one criticism that we might make is that it offers only a partial picture. We consider which groups have capacity, assess the relative weight of other connections and assign responsibilities to remedy to groups to provide support today. But what of the long-term? Consider *Evil Nation* (Brooks 2011:199–200). Evil Nation desires and attempts to create severe poverty elsewhere at every opportunity. It has causal, moral, and outcome responsibility – and perhaps draws some benefit from its actions. However, it lacks any means of remedy. What to do?

The problem for Miller's connection theory is that it lacks a mechanism to hold Evil Nation to account. It can never be required to provide remedies because, say, it never has the capacity. It falls to other groups to continually provide support and assistance to those groups harmed by Evil Nation. What this shows is that while Miller's theory is enormously useful for thinking about how to assign responsibilities here and now, it lacks some follow-up position about ensuring justice is done post-rescues.

Capabilities

A common view of improving international development is to focus on resources-only. When a country's Gross Domestic Product (GDP) improves, this is taken to be evidence that the country is improving and escaping severe poverty. However, GDP measures the *average* wealth in a community which can mask deep inequalities. For example, country A might have a GDP at just below securing everyone's basic needs. Suppose country A's wealth was distributed equally. Country B's GDP is slightly higher and, as an average, appears to meet the minimum required to secure basic needs – and so an improvement on country A. However, country B has a destitute citizenry living in severe poverty, but the country's average wealth is much higher because the country's ruling class is incredibly rich. This example shows that a higher GDP is not necessarily evidence that a society's population overall has more resources.

In contrast, Amartya Sen developed the capability approach. He argues we should think about development primarily in terms of freedom – in what individuals can do or be – rather than GDP as a better measure of progress. Sen (1999:20) claims when we think about development it must be in terms of "basic capabilities" measured by premature mortality, significant malnourishment (especially of children), persistent morbidity, widespread illiteracy, and other failures. Furthermore, he provides empirical evidence that improvements in these areas is not always linked to having greater affluence. In fact, wealthier groups can perform worse than others – with the real link being a lack of capabilities (Sen 1999:22–23).

While Sen noticeably rejects setting out a list of capabilities or demarking a threshold that they must meet or surpass, this is exactly what Martha Nussbaum defends. She argues that there are ten capabilities that must all be satisfied at or above a threshold:

1. *Life*: the ability to live a human life of normal length and worth living;
2. *Bodily health*: the ability to be adequately nourished, possess adequate shelter, and maintain good health, including reproductive health;
3. *Bodily integrity*: the ability to move freely, being secure against violent assault, having opportunities for sexual satisfaction, and reproductive choice;
4. *Senses, imagination, and thought*: the ability to receive an adequate education, possessing freedom of expression and religious exercise, being able to experience literary or musical works or events, and the ability to have pleasurable experiences;
5. *Emotions*: the ability to have attachments to things and people outside of ourselves, to love those who love and care for us, and not have our emotional development stunted by fear or anxiety;
6. *Practical reason*: the ability to form conceptions of the good and engage in critical reflection in planning one's life;
7. *Affiliation*: (A) the ability to live with and toward others, engaging in social interactions; (B) the ability to have the social bases of self-respect and non-humiliation, being treated as a dignified person of equal worth, and nondiscrimination on the basis of race, sex, sexual orientation, ethnicity, caste, religion, or national origin;
8. *Other species*: the ability to live with concern for and in relation to plant and animal species;
9. *Play*: the ability to laugh, play, and enjoy recreational activities; and
10. *Control over one's environment*: (A) *Political*: the ability to participate effectively in political choices, enjoying protections of free speech and association; (B) *Material*: the ability to have property rights on an

equal basis with others, the right to seek employment on an equal basis with others, and freedom from unwarranted search and seizure (Nussbaum 2011:33–34).

Each capability on the list is of central importance and has equal weight. Nussbaum denies that any one capability (e.g. to life) is more valuable than another (e.g. to play). Every capability must be available for any individual to exercise with the same opportunities to do so (Nussbaum 2000:74, 81).

Crucially, everyone must be able to exercise their capabilities at or above a minimum threshold. Otherwise, a sufficient minimal level of justice is not secured. Capabilities are meant to capture human well-being and when any one of them is denied our dignity and rights are not achieved (Nussbaum 2011:36). There can be no trade-offs either: an excess of one capability does not make up for falling below a threshold in another. Ultimately, "it is for the government to secure them, if that government is to be even minimally just" (Nussbaum 2011:36).

The capabilities approach is a highly influential alternative to the standard view that development is primarily about resources. While resources are undoubtedly important, the capabilities approach refocuses our attention on improvements in people's freedoms to do or be, such as in relation to Nussbaum's list. When considering how to improve the lives of individuals in developing countries, the capabilities approach advocates a compelling view that conditions are better – not necessarily because there is higher average wealth, but – when lives are lived with dignity, with opportunities to secure bodily health and other goods and where there is genuine, material choice.

One issue to note that the use of lists – such as of 10 (or more) capabilities – may appear somewhat unwieldy and overly complex, especially in light of the fact there is a recognized overlap between some of them (Nussbaum 2011:21–24). Thom Brooks agrees with Nussbaum's list, but argues it could be reorganized into three groups of capabilities (dividing Nussbaum's list between them as (sub)capabilities). For example:

1. *Body*: the ability to achieve (sub)capabilities of life and bodily health;
2. *Brain*: the ability to achieve (sub)capabilities of senses, imagination, and thought; emotions and practical reason; and
3. *Boundaries*: the ability to achieve (sub)capabilities of bodily integrity, affiliation, other species, play and control over one's environment (Brooks 2020c:204–205).

This shorter list of three capability group is meant to serve two goals. First, it is to make it easier to apply with a more focused list. We consider how individuals meet a satisfactory threshold in terms of their "body" (noting our physiological needs as a living organism), "brain" (noting our cognitive development and practical reasoning abilities) and "boundaries" (noting our relations to others and to our political and natural world). Second, in a significant difference from Nussbaum, each grouping marks out a progressively wider concentric circle of importance. The capability group of our body is essential to secure to enjoy any other capability grouping. While the body capability group makes possible the exercise of the brain and practical reasoning group, this group, in turn, allows us to make possible the pursuit of our capability group of boundaries.

This ordering highlights the links connecting one group to the next, but it does not claim that we can satisfactorily achieve a life of dignity meeting a threshold of one or two groups and not all. Like Nussbaum, Brooks argues all capabilities must be secured in a similar way. But this capability group model aims at making it easier to apply and to understand how different capabilities relate to one another.

Realism and practical matters

Our discussion about duties, remedial responsibilities and even capabilities has been about the application of theories to practice. We develop a view, say, of negative duty and then reflect on what consequences flow from it. Now let us consider the reverse – the application of practice to theories – and their possible relevance. It is a truism that our world is not perfectly just, but what does this reality mean for theorizing about global justice?

Thomas Nagel (2005:113) argues that the "most important current task" for political philosophers is finding "workable ideas about the global or international" sphere.[13] Nagel (2005:147) accepts Hobbes' view that states are sovereign operating in an anarchic global order without any world government. Nagel's argument is that our journey "from anarchy to justice must go through injustice." Controversially, he claims we must – in some sense – allow things to get worse before they improve by prioritizing *effective* institutions over *legitimate* institutions (Nagel 2005:147).

Nagel says that, in world politics, global institutions are under pressure to strengthen the protection of human rights, to provide humanitarian assistance where needed and develop global public

---

[13] See *The Global Justice Reader*, chapter 23.

goods benefiting everyone, such as free trade, collective security, and environmental protections. He says:

> Institutions that serve these purposes are not designed to extend democratic legitimacy and socioeconomic justice, but they naturally give rise to claims for both, in respect to their design and functioning. And they put pressure on national sovereignty by their need for power to be effective. They thus present a clearly perceived threat to the limits on claims of justice imposed by the political conception. (Nagel 2005:136)

By its nature, global politics aims to secure these various benefits. In doing so, they make possible the extension of legitimacy through social democratic justice. The issue is if we fail to establish sufficiently effective institutions in our drive for more legitimacy for them, this might, in Nagel's view, undermine and restrict their effectiveness – putting both workable institutions and their longer-term legitimacy in jeopardy.

Moreover, Nagel argues we must separate the roles and aims of different levels of governance. At the domestic level, sovereign states are responsible to their citizens and in support of their social justice. But at the global level, this "global or regional network does not have a similar responsibility of social justice for the combined citizenry of all the states involved, a responsibility that if it existed would have to be exercised collectively by the representatives of the member states" (Nagel 2005:139–140). Each state seeks ways of cooperating with others to achieve their individual goals – in the pursuit of making them effective and deliverable. Justice applies in different ways for each level, as each has a different kind of character – and where distributive justice is effectively relegated to the domestic level.

Nagel's views have come under criticism. Philosophers have questioned whether his depiction of how global institutions work is mistaken (see Armstrong 2012:98). A very different view of how practices matter for global justice is developed by Andrea Sangiovanni (2016).[14] He begins by asking the question: "to what extent and in what sense should principles of political morality be responsive to facts about social practices?" (Sangiovanni 2016:4). While it may be obvious that facts about our practices matter for *implementing* some theoretical view, it is much less clear how these facts should shape the development of our theories themselves – and this is what his important contribution attempts to achieve.

Sangiovanni argues that the justification, formulation, and grounding of principles depends on our practices – they are *practice-dependent*. One

---

[14] See *The Global Justice Reader*, chapter 24.

example is grounding a principle. This is where "a principle of political morality … might bind people when and because they are joint participants either in a social practice or in social interaction independent of practice" (Sangiovanni 2016:5). This would arise where we considered a principle about distributing goods to individuals if, and only if, and because, they are conationals. The shared nationality of individuals grounds the principle that applies to them. What matters for this relational approach is that there are conationals fitting this description in the world. Otherwise, the principle would be invalid as it would lack a ground.

Next Sangiovanni considers how our social practices can justify principles. He explains his view through an example. He imagines that we were unable to decide on whether to support a utilitarian or Kantian position to prohibit slavery. Sangiovanni claims that most versions of utilitarianism would likely reject the practice. But there might be some possible formulation where general happiness for the majority sufficiently outweighs the horror experienced by those enslaved – and so justify the practice, at least in principle. In contrast, Kantianism endorses a universal moral law and the equal dignity of all is inviolable. Imagine our choice of which view – utilitarianism or Kantian – is premised on our full commitment to the prohibition of slavery. In that case, we would endorse Kantianism over utilitarianism. Sangiovanni (2016:13) claims that "our considered conviction that slavery is wrong in every possible world … provides us with *evidence* that the Kantian [position] is true." Our conviction about practices does not ground our position, but it does restrict which views we could justify (e.g. a view that prohibited slavery under every circumstance).

Sangiovanni rightly notes that some political philosophers claim that our theories should be more responsive to facts about the social practices to which they are intimately bound up: after all, political philosophy is about theorizing relating to institutions (Brooks 2024). Social practices can and do matter for the grounding and justification of work in areas like global justice. As seen above with Nagel, practice-dependent views depend not only on practices but also our *understanding* of practices as part of the explanatory power behind a practice-dependent position is the fact-dependence of the practice. If practices were not as described or understood, this would necessarily undermine the compelling-power of our position.

Rectificatory justice

We have discussed associative duties for *individuals* arising from their relations to others, such as national group membership. Lea Ypi, Robert Goodin, and Christian Barry (2009) reflect on the "associative relation" of *states* in relation to colonial histories.[15] They point out that a strong view of cosmopolitanism would hold that duties and responsibilities would hold the same for all states. In contrast, associative relations are thought to create different, special duties.

They claim that not all associative relations are the same. There is a cooperative agreement where individuals in relation create associative duties through their cooperative interaction. This is very much the model for liberal nationalists in Chapter 4. A second form is a coercive account where a coercive relation gives rise to special duties, but in a more negative sense.

One example of a coercive-brand of associative duties is colonialism. This is where a colonized state has associative duties arising from its coercive relations with its mother country. For instance, "people in the colonies are often treated differently under the same laws, they are often subject to different laws altogether; typically the even have a wholly different legal status" (Ypi, Goodin, and Barry 2009:110). Their being under a colonial power restricting, if not wholly preventing, their right as a group to self-determination is, of course, an important wrong arising from this coercive relationship.

Ypi, Goodin, and Barry (2009:119) claim that "there are various ways in which those linked by systems of colonialism can be said to be engaged in cooperation in some joint venture sufficient to ground associative duties." For instance, there will be strong reciprocal relations in the joint engagement in production in cooperative trade relations. These can go as far as instilling a kind of anxiety in the colonized state about its independence for fear that whatever positive outcomes from cooperative trade and relations – notwithstanding colonialization – might become severed and so breaking free would lead to their becoming broke.

However, as Ypi, Goodin, and Barry are keen to point out, the associative duties between the colony and its mother state do create special duties. In this case, they create what is called a duty to rectificatory justice that can go both ways. Ypi, Goodin, and Barry (2009:134) argue:

> rich colonies and rich people in the colonies can thereby end up owing associative duties of robust distributive justice to poor people in other colonies or, indeed, in the Mother Country itself. If colonial rule brings colonizers and all the colonized together under the same coercive state apparatus, and if as on the Coercion Account that is what it takes to generate associative duties that give rise to the duties of robust

---

[15] See *The Global Justice Reader*, chapter 225.

distributive justice, then comparable tax-transfer arrangements and other institutions required to satisfy robust principles of distributive justice should operate uniformly across the entire empire, applying identically to each member of that political association wherever he or she lives within the empire.

We might assume at first that any colonial relationship under coercion would necessarily require some rectificatory justice from the mother country to the coerced colony. This may often be true where colonies are exploited in their coercive relationship to the benefit of the mother country. Ypi, Goodin, and Barry's original contribution is recognizing that, through the associative duties shared, rectificatory justice could, under specific conditions, go the other way flowing from the more wealthy colony to the less affluent mother country and its poorer people. Associative duties can take cooperative or coercive shapes – and their special duties can flow either way.

Conclusion

When we think about global justice, we most often think of the problem of global poverty. While everyone seeks to end severe poverty in the world, there is deep disagreement about how we might go about it. In this chapter, we have considered different views on duties. We might claim a positive duty to act where we can – or a negative duty to correct some wrong we are responsible for bringing about. Alternatively, we might bring these together into a connection theory of remedial responsibility, where our aim is to weigh different connections between groups and those in urgent need.

These views are often presented about rescuing others, such as through sharing resources. A different option is to consider development in terms of freedom and capabilities instead of as money. The capabilities approach is a way of focusing on outcomes relating to well-being seemingly missed or uncaptured by most duties-related approaches.

All those positions develop duties and approach to be applied. But, as we have seen, our social practices can matter to both the ground and justification of the views we defend. We have also considered how differences in how we might understand the domestic level versus the global institutional level can influence the future possibilities of putting our theories in practice. Moreover, the relation of states to each other, such as within colonization, can shape the kinds of associative duties they might have to each other.

In these various ways, global poverty is one of our world's greatest ills. The need to address it is incredibly urgent. Throughout this chapter we have surveyed a wide range of different views that help us think about the issues, limitations, and options more carefully.

Discussion questions

1. Which duty is more compelling: positive duties or negative duties?
2. Is Miller's connection theory the most compelling view of assigning remedial responsibilities?
3. Which is best for thinking about alleviating severe poverty: the focus on duties, the focus on resources or the focus on capabilities?
4. Should our practices matter for global justice? If so, how?
5. When, if ever, might a colony owe anything to its parent country?

8

Just War

Introduction

It is a sad reality that war has been a part of human civilization since its origins. Whatever their cause or aim, lives are put at risk or lost, homes and livelihoods imperilled or destroyed, and peoples displaced. A *just war* tradition has evolved over time that sets out the relevant tests that must be met for any war to be deemed "just," or, in other words, to be justified. A key purpose behind such criteria for any justified military conflict is to ensure a high bar is met to constrain states from engaging in war giving the high costs in lives, livelihoods, and much more when they happen.

This chapter will survey some of the leading contributions in just war theory. It will begin with its *premodern* beginnings in the work of the Catholic saint and theologian Thomas Aquinas. While various theorists have reformulated his ideas since, Aquinas's argument for when a war might be just has exerted a long-lasting influence since.

We next consider what is described as the modern *conventional* view. This position revises Aquinas's criteria for a just war amending and recasting it for contemporary times. We will also consider arguments for the principle of nonintervention, the prohibition of targeting innocent civilians, and the moral equality of combatants.

Global Justice: An Introduction, First Edition. Thom Brooks.
© 2023 John Wiley & Sons Ltd. Published 2023 by John Wiley & Sons Ltd.

This is followed by what will be described as the new *revisionist* challenging the mainstream view of just war theory in dominance. This newer group is led by the work of Jeff McMahan, in a more explicitly moral philosophical approach to just war theorizing. The chapter concludes with some reflections on whether, in light of these contributions, it makes best sense to claim wars can be just – or merely excused.

Premodern just war theory

St. Thomas Aquinas's work on just war theory has exercised a powerful influence many centuries later. His views are expressed in his multivolume work *Summa Theologiae* (or "Summary of Theology") and presented in a format that will be unfamiliar for most readers (Aquinas 2002).[1] The relevant section on war lists a number of challenging questions (listed as an "articulus") such as "whether it is always a sin to wage war" or "whether it is lawful to kill the innocent" (Aquinas 2002:240). These are each followed by a consideration of possible objections to what is proposed (listed as "objectio") followed by Aquinas's replies to these objections (listed as "responsio" and occasional additional comments listed as "ad"). While the format (and undoubtedly the terminology) is an unusual format, it does offer a crisp, argument-focused, and considered discussion of a wide range of key points concerning how a just war might be justified.

Aquinas articulates three conditions for a just war. First, there must be *just government*. The government (or, as Aquinas says, "the prince") is entrusted with the protection of its country. It is lawful for them, he claims, "to use the material sword in defense of the commonwealth against those who trouble it from within ... [and] against enemies from without" (Aquinas 2002:240). In contrast, an unjust state would lack legitimacy in defending its rule from seditious forces within or its enemies abroad. This first condition is important as it makes clear that only a just government can wage a just war whatever the circumstances.

The second condition that must be met for a just war is there must be a *just cause*. Aquinas says that those who we fight against "must deserve to have war waged against them because of some wrongdoing" (Aquinas 2002:240). For evidence, he cites the support of St. Augustine of Hippo, whose work influenced Aquinas, who claims a just cause is met when its opponent "has neglected either to put right the wrongs done by its

---

[1] See The Global Justice Reader, chapter 26.

people or to restore what it has unjustly seized" (Aquinas 2002:240). The second condition specifies that a just war must have a just cause. A state cannot launch an offensive for any reason it wishes to.

The third condition for a just war is that it must only be found with a *just intent*. Aquinas defines a just intent for a just war as simply an intention to either "promote a good cause or avert an evil" (Aquinas 2002:241). He is clear that a just government with a just cause cannot be held to fight a just war if its intentions are mostly malign (or "wicked" (Aquinas 2002:241)). War will lead to harms, including the deaths of soldiers and civilians alike. But a just war does not set out with, quoting from Augustine again, "the desire to do harm" (Aquinas 2002:241). The just war is only waged "to secure peace" and bring an end to conflict.

Aquinas says no evil can be done even for the sake of a good end (Aquinas 2002:240).This raises the issue of whether even the purely accidental killing of innocent civilians when aiming at a military target might render such an attack unjust and so unjustified. Aquinas (2002:261) makes two points. First, he says that "which is done according to the order of justice is not a sin." Our intentions must be wholly just and with a just aim in mind. Second, we must give consideration "to what is essential rather than accidental" (Aquinas 2002:262). If our focused intention is on an essential military target against the backdrop of a just war, it might transpire that innocent lives may be lost. Aquinas's point is that this does not undermine the justness of our intent where such happenings are "accidental" and a tangential side-effect of our intended action.

This is the premodern origin of *the doctrine of double effect*. Consider there is a warehouse nearby. It is being used to create weapons to continue an unprovoked attack on your community. You have in possession a bomb that could destroy the warehouse and end production of weapons used in an unjust war against your community. However, there is a canteen serving the soldiers food that is staffed by civilian. Would we be justified in destroying the warehouse knowing it would kill innocent civilians in the process?

The doctrine of double effect would justify bombing the warehouse. The intention is directed at preventing serious harms by ending the production of weapons used to wage an unjust war. While the canteen civilian staff members are not a target, their deaths are an unintended side-effect. They are not the target and the action would be unjustified if the intention is to do them harm. Our action has a *double effect*. The first effect is intended: the destruction of the warehouse. The second effect is unintended: the deaths of innocent civilians.

Conventional just war theory

Aquinas's contributions to just war theory are profound. He argues that war must meet specified conditions for it to be "just" or otherwise any action taken is wrongful. These conditions consist of a just government, a just cause, and a just intent. Moreover, Aquinas also offers core concepts for just war theorizing like the doctrine of double effect. Much of what has come afterward are revisions of what we might call *the core model* of just war theory defended by Aquinas.

For example, John Stuart Mill (1984) carefully considers the issue of having a just cause.[2] Mill observes the truism that any decision to enter into war can have grave consequences. It is crucial that any such move is considered most carefully as lives – including the life of the state – can be put at risk.

Mill's urge for caution is exacerbated by the concern that the rules of war and international law more generally are not equally recognized by all states. Mill (1984:118) is concerned that "the rules of ordinary international morality imply reciprocity. But barbarians will not reciprocate." This further complicates the difficulty of foreseeing the consequences of our actions if we entered into a conflict given some states, but not all, may have regard to ordinary international morality and the rules of war.

One difference between Aquinas and Mill is that Mill claims we should recognize a general principle of nonintervention. His thoughts focus on what he calls "barbarian" states characterized as undemocratic and despotic. We will feel pressure to take action in order to rescue people from their illegitimate and possibly even dangerous government. This will be felt all the stronger if we are certain we could remove a government by military force and hand power over their territory to the people. It may even seem as morally compelling.

However, Mill cautions us against this. He says:

> No people ever was and remained free, but because it was determined to be so ... for, unless the spirit of liberty is strong in a people, those who have the executive in their hands easily work any institutions to the purposes of despotism. (Mill 1984:122–123)

The idea is that an external state cannot make people free on a sustainable basis. Overthrowing an illegitimate government run by one group does not guarantee that another group will be able to do much better. For Mill, we

---

[2] See *The Global Justice Reader*, chapter 27.

do more harm than good in intervening abroad out of a desire to improve lives – and should instead remain focused on military action generally only when required for self-defense.

The principle of noninterference unless in self-defense has found its way into international law. The UN *Charter* (1946) states that it is its Security Council that "shall determine the existence of any threat to the peace, breach of the peace, or act of aggression" making recommendations on how "international peace and security" can be maintained.[3] Importantly, many of the measures listed that the Security Council might recommend involving economic sanctions or disruption of transportation and severing diplomatic relations.[4] It is only when those nonmilitary measures are considered "inadequate or have proved to be inadequate" that military action might be considered "as may be necessary to maintain or restore international peace and security."[5]

The UN's *Charter* also states that it does not impair "the inherent right of individual or collective self-defense if an armed attack occurs against a Member of the United Nations, until the Security Council has taken measures necessary to maintain international peace and security."[6] While the UN's Security Council makes recommendations on how the world community – through the United Nations – attempts to secure global peace, every member state is a sovereign state with a right to defend itself from attack by others until the Security Council is able to intervene. There is an implicit principle of nonintervention where it might threaten the peace among states – and no right of intervening military in any UN member state because it is thought the people would be happier or more prosperous if their government was overthrown.

The statement of these principles does not mean that they are always adhered to. Security Council recommendations on when and how to intervene have been at times highly controversial, and, some might argue, counterproductive. Notwithstanding how states have engaged with the *Charter*, it does again mark out some important features. First, there is no mention of the need for a just government. Second, Aquinas's other just war conditions appear intact: there must be cause relating to a breach of international peace and security and the way any potential conflict is

---

[3] See Chapter VII, Article 39. UN *Charter* is included in *The Global Justice Reader*, chapter 28.
[4] UN *Charter*, Chapter VII, Article 41.
[5] UN *Charter*, Chapter VII, Article 42.
[6] UN *Charter*, Chapter VII, Article 51.

handed should be done with a just intent to secure a sustainable peace. Aquinas's core model influences us several centuries later.

Thomas Nagel (1972) argues for the importance of having rules of war that are "absolutist." By this, he means universally held principles that are without exceptions.[7] This is a focus on the idea of having a *just intent*. Nagel (1972:124) claims we must set clear parameters on the conduct of war – to prevent atrocities and war crimes by countries taking a means-justifies-the-ends approach to war. We should endorse a prohibition on targeting civilians without exceptions.[8]

It is easy to imagine a country engaged in war – whether justly or not – and, fearing for its likely defeat, decides on a steep escalation in violence, such as towards civilians, to improve its military fortunes. Nagel claims an absolutist prohibition would make clear that any such targeting of civilians is morally unjustifiable and worthy of condemnation. But he is careful to note that his absolutist prohibition is only on the deliberate targeting of civilians. Its focus is on what we *do* and not what might *result*. He acknowledges that his views are compatible with the doctrine of double effect as the death of innocents as an unintended side-effect is not prohibited (Nagel 1972:130).

Nagel's prohibition also has the benefit that we need not risk opening a Pandora's box to possible gross injustices, such as bombing civilian cities in order to gain an advantage in military strategy. Targeting civilians in combat is something that should never be done. For Nagel, this fact is intuitive because we do not believe that such an action is capable of justification. It is not a question of ends justifying the means, but rather that some means are wholly illegitimate and wrong, no matter the ends.

There is a further principle to consider – that of the *moral symmetry of combatants*. The modern conventional view in just war theory is that we can conceptually separate the *jus ad bellum* (or "the justifiability of the war" such as its just cause that could justify going to war) from the *jus in bello* (or "the conduct of warring parties" relating to their proportionate actions when at war and discriminating between combatants and noncombatants). While just war theorists would normally claim that any "just war" must satisfy both a just cause and a just intention, they are considered separately. The one does not alter the other beyond the fact both must be separately satisfied to justify a military attack. Note again that the need for a just government – proposed by Aquinas – is not a part of the conventional just war doctrine.

---

[7] See *The Global Justice Reader*, chapter 29.
[8] For a collection of insightful essays on civilian immunity in war, see Primoratz (2007).

Michael Walzer (2000:34, 41) argues for the moral symmetry of combatants. He claims they have "moral equality" when in combat with "an equal right to kill."[9] Imagine two soldiers confronting each other on the field of battle during a war. To make clear the unambiguous goodness of one and badness of the other, let us suppose one is a jedi knight who has a just cause and, in following "the force," always fights with just intention to secure peace. Their opponent is an imperial stormtrooper on orders of an evil emperor who lacks just cause and whose side does not fight with good intent.

According to Walzer, the different statuses of their having a just or unjust cause is irrelevant in this scenario. Each is in a virtual state of nature. Each puts their life at risk in engaging in combat and so, for Walzer, both have a right to self-defense in response to any attack. The jedi is no more justified in defending their life with potentially lethal force than the stormtrooper. They both have moral equality – and their position is symmetrical. Whatever their cause, each may be attacked by the other and defend their own right to life.

Revisionist just war theory

Over the last two decades, there has been a growing movement in just war theory that has become the new orthodoxy. Inspired predominantly by the fascinating work of Jeff McMahan (2009), most just war theorists today broadly work within the framework McMahan sets out which has – without any exaggeration – revolutionized an otherwise fairly conservative field.[10]

In his "revisionist" account of just war theory, McMahan (2005:55) recasts its traditional roots in fundamental ways.[11] He notes that conventional just war theory holds that a just cause is a necessary condition, among others, for resorting to war. McMahan (2005:56) claims most theorists make the mistake of thinking this condition can only apply to the initial decision to go to war – and that afterwards our focus turns away from the just cause to other factors, such as whether we conduct ourselves with just intent during the war itself. This is a mistake because a war can, McMahan says, begin without a just cause but acquire one later during the fighting. If that happened, it would be absurd to say that during the battle an unjust war ended so a just war could launch. Likewise, we could start with a just

---

[9] See Kant (1996:117) [§57: 6:347]

[10] For a collection of papers mostly working within this new orthodoxy framework engaged with McMahan's revolution, see Brooks (2013c).

[11] See *The Global Justice Reader*, chapter 30.

cause but then see its just status change during battle, such as when this just cause has been achieved or disappeared on its own.

McMahan's (2005:56) point is that "a just cause is, indeed, always required for engaging in warm," but *also* for the "continuation of war." Thus, he defends the admittedly "highly unorthodox claim" that a just cause is required to justify both the decision to go to war (the *jus ad bellum*) and the continuation of that war (the *jus in bello*).[12] This is stark contrast to the then orthodox view, as defended by Walzer (2000:21), that *jus ad bellum* and *jus in bello* are "logically independent" and can be considered separately. McMahan rejects this separation.

Moreover, a just cause dictates, in part, the conduct of war. As noted, the status of whether we have a just cause determines whether our war is just or unjust. When a just cause is no more, any just war waged loses its justification. For example, when the military objective is achieved there is no justification for one's side to continue fighting – they have lost their just cause and must cease their fight (McMahan 2005:61).

McMahan next challenges the conventional view of the moral symmetry of combatants. McMahan (2005:62) considers our liability to be attacked and says:

> Here, then, is a statement of the formal concept of just cause. There is just cause for war when one group of people – often a state, but possibly a nation or other organized collective – is morally responsible for action that threatens to wrong or has already wronged other people in certain ways, and that makes the perpetrators liable to military attack as a means of preventing the threatened wrong or redressing or correcting the wrong that has already been done.

McMahan sets up a dichotomy between the just and unjust combatant. The unjust combatant is morally responsible for actions that threaten to do wrongs or have wronged already. This makes them liable to military attack to prevent or redress their wrongful conduct. But, for McMahan, this is untrue of just combatants who are not liable to be attacked. Despite the fact a just combatant may pose a threat and harm opponents, "they oppose the military action of unjust combatants" and so "do not thereby become legitimate targets of attack but retain their innocence in the generic sense" (McMahan 2009:14).

---

[12] On the different parts of *jus ad bellum* and *jus in bello*, see Guthrie and Quinlan (2007:12–14).

McMahan argues for the *moral asymmetry of combatants*. He says that "combatants who fight for a cause that is just or good but whose war is nevertheless unjustified do not have the same moral status as just combatants" (McMahan 2009:6). McMahan (2009:9, 57) argues that, in being an unjust combatant, I make myself liable to attack from others because, in acting unjustly, I lose my right to defend myself.

Therefore, "not all combatants are legitimate targets of attack in war" (McMahan 2009:204). Unjust combatants ought not fight even if commanded to do so (McMahan 2005:63; McMahan 2009:95–98). McMahan rejects the idea that simply posing a threat to others makes them necessarily liable to attack. He says that, if this were true, then individuals engaged in self-defense render themselves liable to attack which is absurd (McMahan 2005:65). What matters is our status as a just or unjust combatant and the moral difference this has.

Within this new orthodox framework, Seth Lazar (2012:4) focuses on the requirement that "the force used must be necessary to avert the threat."[13] Just as an individual's right to self-defense must be both proportionate and necessary, so too in this framework must a state's just cause be proportionate and necessary. In this way, establishing necessity is essential to justifying both self-defense and war.

For self-defense to be proportionate, it must not be more severe than is required to protect oneself from attack. We can only use as little harm as is required – what is necessary – to protect ourselves from attack. If we have been attacked and the attack is over, then, for Lazar, it is no longer necessary for us to take defensive action. While striking back *might* have been justified during the attack to stop it, it is *not* justified after it is over.

Moreover, our judgment about proportionality and necessity is "evidence-relative" (Lazar 2012:8). If someone attacked us and we struck back, but – unbeknownst to us – there was a button in front of us that would drop a glass cage imprisoning our attacker unharmed, the least harmful option is to press the button. Lazar (2012:7–8) says it matters whether we are aware as our judgments of just or unjust action can only be based on the evidence available to us at the time.

Conventional just war theory and what we might call *the revisionist turn* have commonalities and differences. They broadly agree on that any just war must satisfy the conditions of *jus ad bellum* and *jus ad bello*. Their disagreement is that conventional just war theorists consider these separate issues whereas revisionists claim they are intrinsically linked. A further

---

[13] See *The Global Justice Reader*, chapter 31.

difference is that conventional just war theorists claim soldiers confronting each other in battle have moral symmetry where each has a right to defend themselves. In contrast, the revisionists claim combatants are either just or unjust with only the just able to engage in attack.

Is war "just"?

We have seen the commonalities and differences between conventional and revisionist just war theories. Perhaps the biggest aspect in common is that both believe war can be "just": those who are justified in engaging in just war do not perform a wrong if satisfying all just war criteria. Let us examine this further with close attention to revisionist just war theory accounts, as these are currently dominant.

Revisionist theories are effectively grounded in a particular view about how self-defense works.[14] The general idea is that just war is a form of defensive killing at the international level similar to the right of individuals to engage in self-defense at the domestic level. For example, I may use potentially lethal force against an unjust aggressor as a private individual. My attacker has no right to injure me with no moral justification for doing so nor to defend himself from my response. Likewise, combatants may justly engage in war against unjust aggressors as part of a state. Unjust combatants have no right to engage militarily with no moral justification for fighting nor defending themselves from my defensive actions. As Lazar (2012:24) says: "The central idea is that precisely the same principles that justify individual self- and other-defense killing in war." McMahan (2009:156) agrees: "The difference between war and other forms of conflict is a difference *only of degree* and this, the moral principles that govern killings in lesser forms of conflict, govern killing in war as well. A state of war *makes no difference* other than to make the application of the relevant principles more complicated and difficult."[15]

There are two objections to the revisionist model. The first is that its view of self-defense is based on a category mistake. What it is to engage in defensive killing as an innocent individual fighting off an attacker is a different thing to defensive killing as a just combatant at war with unjust combatants. For example, individuals are engaged in an act of self-defense in a direct response to an immediate threat. The individual does not normally

---

[14]This view currently dominates philosophical discussion of war's morality" (Lazar 2012:25).

[15]Emphasis added.

choose the timing for when defensive action happens – it takes place when I am under threat. The purpose of my action is to end the immediate threat either through violence, escaping or some other means. This is a very different situation from combatants at war. Just combatants act on behalf of a state responding to a macro-threat from an enemy state, not starting from an immediate threat. The just combatant enters conflict to end it whereas the citizen non-combatant seeks to end or escape the immediacy of threat to them (Lazar 2012:27, 39). In the one case, individuals seek exit so the state can intervene; but, in the second case, states seek to enter as there is no world-state or global police to intervene instead. The two kinds of cases understand self-defense in very different ways.

The second objection is that, if we wanted to draw on *individual* self-defense as our archetype for *international* self-defense in war, we accept a very different view of what self-defense is and how it works. To explain, let us consider McMahan's distinction between justification and excuse:

> *Justification*: an act is justified if and only if it is permissible in the circumstances *and* there is positive moral reason to do it. (McMahan 2009:110)[16]

> *Excuse*: when an act is wrong but the agent who does it is not blameworthy, he or she is excused. (McMahan 2009:110)

McMahan's argument is that self-defense is a kind of *justification*. He claims that when I exercise a right to self-defense in war my actions are justified if a just combatant. In fact, the idea that self-defense could act as an excuse is a view mostly discussed in terms of excusing the activities of unjust combatants (McMahan 2009:115–154, 182–189).

The problem with this view of self-defense as a justification, not an excuse, is that it is inconsistent with how the right of self-defense works in most criminal law systems.[17] In domestic law, the right of self-defense serves as a possible defense – an excuse – against prosecution for what

---

[16] Emphasis given.

[17] There is the famous example from Kant of two shipwrecked castaways. Imagine that you are in a shipwreck. You are clinging to a plank. The only way that you might stay afloat is if you push someone else clinging to this plank off it – and they would drown. Kant (1996:28) says such an action is *culpable* but not *punishable*. The reason is that killing anyone is always wrong, but this action is not punishable because it is excused. This is on the basis that the certainty of death from drowning if you do not save yourself is less than the certainty of punishment – and so a case of acting under extreme duress that absolves one of criminal responsibility.

might otherwise have been a crime.[18] Punching someone could be prosecuted for battery or a more serious crime depending on the impact to the individual punched. But if there is defense like acting in self-defense, then prosecution is avoided and innocence secured.

McMahan acknowledges his awareness that his *moral theory* about how self-defenses work is different from their *legal status*. He says: "the notion of justification *in the law* is, of course, slightly different from my under-standing of *moral justification*" (McMahan 2009:44).[19] His hope is that the law will be reformed noting "it is imperative that we work to bring the *law* of war into closer conformity with the *morality* of war" (McMahan 2009:107, see 109, 126).[20]

One issue with this aspiration is that the legal view of self-defense as an excuse is not minority view in most legal systems – it is commonplace and nor is the idea of self-defense as an excusing defense to prosecution new either. So, there is a possible disagreement here about whether the conventional view rooted in the law across jurisdictions for decades is preferable to a new normative theory and why.

But a second issue – if we side with theory over an established view of self-defense in law – is McMahan claims that the standard we should follow is objective. McMahan (2009:113) says: "duress it not a justification nor does it ground a permission – not even a subjective permission. It is, instead, an excusing condition." Referring to "objective wrongdoing" (2009:155) he also says that: "excuses reduce the degree of a person's responsibility for action that is *objectively* wrong" (2009:155, 192).

Duress in criminal law is normally a subjective test about whether someone had a reasonable belief about being in danger. It is described as: "the person acting under duress has done the wrong thing, and yet cannot be held responsible (or blamed) for doing what they did ... the person excused under duress was forced to make the wrong choice, and in this sense made no choice at all" (Dubber 2015:182). An individual under attack and afraid for their well-being strikes an attacker. In normal circumstances, striking another is a crime. But if an individual could be reasonably found to be under duress, there is no crime to be prosecuted for an act that is otherwise an offense.

The point is not to argue for one or the other view of self-defense. The strength of the revisionist view of just war theory is in its understanding

---

[18] See Lazar (2012:6).
[19] Emphasis added.
[20] Emphasis added.

and use of self-defense in fleshing out its claims. I have only drawn attention to how this moralized view of self-defense – on which so much is built – is different in some significant ways to self-defense's common legal under-standing. A strict reading of using the legal model for individual self-defense as a model for international cases of self-defense might suggest that just war theory is best understood as a theory of excusing, not necessarily justifying, actions that are otherwise wrongful. If we are satisfied by the revisionist position but not this implication relating to grounding its view in individual self-defense, then revisionist adherents might retain their view – but not claim it is based on an extension of interactions between individuals within a state.

The moral symmetry of noncombatants

We have seen the debate over the moral symmetry – or asymmetry – of combatants. The conventional view is combatants are moral symmetrical with an equal right to defend themselves in battle no matter which side they are on. The revisionist view is that combatants are morally asymmetrical where only just combatants can attack. But what about non-combatants?

One of the most interesting discussions of this issue is offered by the French existentialist Albert Camus (1986).[21] He argues that every military conflict leads to the deaths of innocent civilians. The noncombatants killed are chosen at random and, as civilians, are morally symmetrical to each other. No one has any more right against being killed as a side effect of war than anybody else.

However, there can be a moral asymmetry between the noncombatant civilian populations on each side. There is a difference between a civilian in a country under attack who supports military action against an attacker and a civilian from that attacking country a safe distance away who supports military action. The difference is the civilian in a state under siege will be more likely, however remotely, to be killed as collateral damage than a civil-ian in a state far beyond where the battle is taking place. For the civilian far away, supporting a military campaign comes without costs – they are safe

---

[21] I discovered this short book in the used books section of a wonderful bookstore in Tempe, Arizona while a MA graduate student at Arizona State University. While I do not agree with all of its arguments, Camus's work can be very useful in considering issues from a different, even unconventional perspective that is thought-provoking.

from attack and any such war support is a matter that may not put themselves in danger like it would others in the country to be attacked.

Camus (1986:30) raises the following questions:

> "Do you or do you not, directly or indirectly, want to be killed or assaulted? Do you or do you not, directly or indirectly, want to kill or assault" All who say No to both these questions are automatically committed to a series of consequences which must modify their way of posing the problem.

The argument in support of a military attack will lead to innocent civilians in the target country being harmed and possibly killed. They have no more right to be killed than we do, but in supporting the action we put them at risk. So, for Camus, he wants us to ask ourselves if we would be willing to be chosen randomly to be harmed or killed in retaliation by our opponent's military. If we are unwilling to put ourselves at such risk in support of a military campaign, then we are morally inconsistent to say that others – with the same moral standing as us – must be put at this risk.

Camus's point is that innocent civilians on both sides have moral symmetry and share the same moral standing. Yet, so often the battle take place at one site impacting the civilians in one place far more than the other. Despite their moral symmetry, there is outcome asymmetry in the personal costs different sides bear. Camus reminds us that our support (or nonsupport) for military action has consequences not only for combatants but civilians too. He urges us to reflect on our shared, equal moral status and try to build a global politics where there are "neither victims nor executioners" (Camus 1986).

Conclusion

Wars have been a tragic part of human civilization since its beginnings. It was said by Bertrand Russell said "war does not determine who is right, only who is left" (Dill 2015:627). Indeed, military scholars admit that just war theory "does not yield a tidy ad unambiguous answer to every question" (Guthrie and Quinlan 2007:46).

This chapter has attempted to survey three broad groups. First, it considered the pre modern conception of just war theory as defended by Aquinas. He claimed that a just war required three conditions to be met – a just government, a just cause and, a just intention – and introduced the doctrine of double effect. Second, we surveyed the main contributions of modern conventional just war theory and its reappropriation of

Aquinas's conditions into two: the *just ad bellum* and *jus in bello*. We noted the principle of noninterference, the prohibition on deliberately targeting civilians and the moral symmetry of combatants. Third, we turned to the new revisionist just war theory based on a particular view of self-defense and its application – and its claim of an asymmetry of combatants between those that are just or unjust. Finally, we noted a few possible objections to these views.

We disagree as much about just war theories as we might the justice of individual military conflicts. This chapter's survey highlights some of the leading contributions to this highly significant, and thought-provoking, area.

Discussion questions

1. What is a just cause that might justify war?
2. What are the limits on a just intent in how a war is fought?
3. Does it matter if a country with a just cause and just intent is an unjust dictatorship?
4. Do combatants in battle have moral symmetry or asymmetry?
5. Is any war "just"?

9

Terrorism

Introduction

Terrorism is not new, but its size, shape, and targets are ever-shifting. The events of 11 September 2001 in the United States have changed many aspects about national security forever. It also had a significant impact on political and legal philosophy. While most philosophical work about global justice focused on different topics, this changed suddenly since 9/11 and interest continues to grow.

Terrorism is not like just war theory. In the latter, we reflect on the reasons for a just cause or the limits for how a war might be fought. There is often an overriding drive to find binding norms or universal principles that could guide global conduct with examples like the UN's *Charter* and international agreements.

But terrorism is different. Terrorist activities force us to reflect carefully on the unthinkable targeting of civilians living everyday lives. Its aims are to secure objectives through violence and fear rather than reason or persuasion – and usually explicitly targeting innocent civilians.

This chapter surveys some of the key contributions to this topic. It will first attempt a definition about what terrorism is and what it hopes to achieve. The next section considers whether we can have terrorism without intending to target civilians. The following section will discuss the

Global Justice: An Introduction, First Edition. Thom Brooks.
© 2023 John Wiley & Sons Ltd. Published 2023 by John Wiley & Sons Ltd.

issues of assassination and targeted killings. The final section considers whether terrorism can ever be justified.

What is terrorism?

Terrorism is defined primarily by what it does: engage in *terror*. It is a terror-creating activity by its very nature and *outcome-oriented*. If an alleged act of "terrorism" failed to create some degree of fear, it would not merit the label.

Terrorism has an object, but this is more difficult to define. In general, it seeks to create terror to achieve some purpose made possible through it. Two specific definitions worth considering are:

Definition 1: The tactic of intentionally targeting non-combatants [or non-combatant property, when significantly related to life and security] with lethal or severe violence ... meant to produce political results via the creation of fear. (Coady 2001:1697)

Definition 2: The deliberate use of violence, or threat of its use, against innocent people, with the aim of intimidating some other people into a course of action they otherwise would not take. (Primoratz 2013:24)

Both definitions see terrorism as (i) deliberate and/or intentional, (ii) targeting innocent noncombatants and (iii) using violence. Where they differ is Coady (2001) claims the end of terrorism is to produce some political result while Primoratz (2013) argues terrorism may be unpolitical and simply seeks to make something happen, as a result of a terrorist activity, that would not otherwise happen.[1]

We might challenge both definitions. First, must terrorism target only civilians and noncombatants? This definition would not include the brutal attack on American marine barracks in Lebanon in 1983. It would also fail to capture the provisional IRA bombing at a hotel in Brighton the following year targeting British Prime Minister Margaret Thatcher who narrowly escaped but Deputy Chief Whip Sir Anthony Berry MP and four others were killed.

Secondly, why think the result – as Coady claims – must be political? Much terrorist activity may seek as its end some change led by political leaders seeking to avert another terrorist incident. But terrorists may seek

---

[1] See also Steinhoff (2007:109–137). Ackerman (2006:13) describes terrorism as "simply the name of a technique: intentional attacks on innocent civilians."

other ends, such as notoriety or power. Terrorists seek to create terror that enables a change, but it need not always be politically-oriented. So, let us work with this definition of terrorism:

> The deliberate threat or use of violence creating fear in order to achieve some outcome.

This definition makes clear that:

1. Terrorism is deliberate,
2. Terrorism is a terror-creating activity,
3. Terror can be created through threats of violence or actual violence,
4. Terrorism seeks to achieve an outcome, and
5. This outcome is to be achieved through terror.

(1) Terrorism is not accidental. While it need not be the product of a well-worked out plan, terrorism requires a deliberate effort. (2) This effort is focused in a terror-creating activity of some kind. If my deliberate plan is to harm and not cause fear, this would be categorized as a non-terrorist activity. A routine element of any terror-creating activity is that the terrorist activity appears random and without warning from the perspective of victims. (3) The activity must involve some threat of violence or actual violence. (4) The purpose for this activity is to achieve some outcome. It does not matter if the outcome is not achieved for it to be considered a terrorist activity. (5) This outcome via the activity is meant to be achieved through terror. It remains terrorism even if the activity is counterproductive in seeking to achieve some end. What matters is the activity seeks to achieve an outcome through terror.

Some argue that "the deliberate killing of innocent people" is an essential aspect of terrorism (Walzer 2002) – and everything hinges on who qualifies as "innocent people." The most common understanding of "innocent people" is as a "noncombatant." This speaks to the distinction in just war theory between combatants actively engaged in battle and the noncombatants who should not be the target of the battle. Some worry that this is too narrow. For example, Virginia Held (2008:17) says that we should not draw a very sharp distinction between events like the 9/11 attack on the World Trade Center targeting mostly civilians and the attack that same day with similar means on the Pentagon targeting the headquarters of the US Department of Defense.

There are two further points to make on this issue. First, the philosophical definition of terrorism must account for real-life cases commonly described as terrorism. Any definition must be both conceptually sound, and capture the variety of different cases and so, in this sense, it is practice-dependent. Second, some philosophers distinguish between the definition of terrorism and the wrongfulness of terrorism. Neither Coady, Primoratz nor my proposed definition states that the activity is always wrong. To include a normative judgement as part of defining the term would be to use a definitional-stop (Hart 2008:5). Terrorism may be always unjustifiable (as discussed later in Chapter 10), but this is thought to be a separate normative assessment about terrorism that comes after our being identify it – and which we should try, however difficult, to consider separately.

Terrorism and intentions

Now that we have reflected on how to *define* terrorism, we turn to the issue of how to *normatively assess* terrorism. Terrorism definitions all describe it as activity that is wrongful in seeking to threaten violence or inflict actual violence to frighten others. David Rodin (2004) attempts to help explain the wrongfulness of terrorism.[2] He does not seek to define terrorism in such a way to capture every possible use, but instead to focus on the distinctive features that figure in our moral thinking.

Rodin identifies four different ways of defining terrorism. The first is called the *tactical and operational* definition. This refers to the weapons and "operational modalities," including military-like practices (Rodin 2004:753). One aspect he singles out is that terrorist violence "comes unpredictably, often without warning," from the perspective of victims (Rodin 2004:754).

The second is the *teleological* definition. This focuses on the ends or goals of the terrorist violence. Rodin notes that the desired outcome can differ widely, but a key element is that, in terrorism, the aim is to produce some outcome through the use of fear. In that sense, "terror" is etymologically and conceptually an essential element of "terrorism" (Rodin 2004:754).

The third way of thinking about terrorism is called the *agent-focused* definition. Rodin notes that some choose to say the relevant agent that undertakes terrorism excludes state actors. Thus, terrorism is not performed by states, but instead "perpetrated ... by sub-national groups or clandestine agents" (Lopez and Gordon 2000:103). But this point is controversial and some have argued that states can and do engage terror-creating activities in conduct that should be considered terrorism.

---

[2] See *The Global Justice Reader*, chapter 32.

The fourth and final way of defining terrorism is the *object-focused* definition. This is where terrorism is defined, in part, in its target. These objects are described variously as "innocent," "neutral," "civilian," or "noncombatant" (Rodin 2004:755).

Rodin observes that each of these different definitions can help us grasp important factors about terrorism across a variety of cases. However, in his view, the most essential factor concerns the object against which terrorist violence or threats is directed. He says: "The key to a moral understanding of terrorism is that it consists in the use of force against those who should not have force used against them" (Rodin 2004:755).

Rodin (2004:755) offers the following moral definition of terrorism:

> Terrorism is the deliberate, negligent, or reckless use of force against noncombatants, by state or nonstate actors for ideological ends and in the absence of a substantively just legal process.

He explains its component parts in the following way. Rodin (2004:755) refers to the "use of force" to capture the coercive nature of terrorism ranging from bombs to booby traps, poisoning to property damage. Rodin claims that this idea is broader than "violence" although this is not obvious.

Perhaps the most controversial element is the definitional inclusion of "ideological ends." Rodin (2004:756) says: "The term 'ideological' is used here in its broadest sense to signify 'a systematic scheme of ideas, usually relating to politics or society, or to the conduct of a class or group, and regarded as justifying actions'." He is keen to distinguish these ends from common criminals. For example, a lone blackmailer might threaten someone with violence if not given a large amount of money. Or a gang may kidnap an individual to get their family to agree a deal for the individual's release. These are both examples where fear and intimidation are used to achieve unlawful goals. But there need not be any wider ideological goal.

Yet, it is unclear that terrorists must have some political treatise to enact or higher goal in mind. To borrow from popular culture, the movie *The Dark Knight* sets Batman against the Joker where the latter and his gang terrorize Gotham City with the aim of spreading fear. When discussing the Joker's motives, Batman's butler Alfred Pennyworth says, "Some people just want to see the world burn" (Nolan 2008). While the Joker is purely fictional, it is not unrealistic to imagine terrorism aiming at an outcome – such as creating chaos or spreading misery – that has no clear ideological commitments. Of course, the Joker's campaign was a series of very serious crimes. But so, too, are international war crimes which might also classify as kinds of terrorism.

Rodin (2004:757) says his inclusion of "noncombatants" as the target of terrorism is "the crux of the argument." He argues:

> Put simply, terrorism involves the use of force against those who should not have force used against them, and to do so is a moral crime. Thus, terrorism is the political or ideological species of common violent crime. It is the criminality (and in its most serious form, the murderousness) of terrorism which explains its moral status and the reaction we rightly have to it. (Rodin 2004:757)

Rodin argues that this captures an important part of our everyday moral thinking, namely, that an ordinary person, not engaged in any threatening combat-like operations should not be a target. His definition clearly includes noncombatant civilians, but his explanation might be thought to extend to non-civilians when not in a combat-like operation – and he positively notes as an example he would include of a bomb attack of a US naval ship (USS *Cole*) staffed by combatants, but who were not engaged in a combat-related mission. While targets can be combatants or noncombatants, similarly Rodin (2004:758) allows for state or non-state actors as the agents of terrorist activity in what he describes as making "the universality of the definition explicit" applying to any group. This is qualified by noting that – whatever else the activity is – it falls outside any substantively just legal process.

The most distinctive aspect of Rodin's view is that he claims both negligent and reckless uses of force can count as terrorism. He notes the doctrine of double effect. If our intention is a morally justifiable action to target a military target, this can be morally acceptable even if there are civilian deaths as an unintended side-effect.

Rodin notes that we would all agree the deliberate targeting of noncombatants, or *terror bombing*, is terrorism and wrongful, but what of negligent or reckless attempts at *targeted killing*? He claims that we can perform targeted killing – such as through drone strikes – in a morally justified way, such as aiming at key tactical targets as just combatants against unjust combatants, even if civilians are killed as an unintended side-effect.

However, this requires that we maintain a "reasonable standard of care" in our actions (Rodin 2004:765). Rodin claims that a high standard is required in the case of activities like targeted killing. This is because of the need to ensure discrimination in ensuring our focus is on combatants and proportionality. If the unintended side-effect of a military operation based on dropping a large bomb on a city killing tens of thousands while knocking out an enemy's telecommunications tower, this would be unjustified as disproportionate to achieving the operational aim. Similarly, if we negligently or recklessly – and so without a reasonable standard of care – order drone strikes that do far more harm to noncombatants than the intended target, then we may not say these are mere unintended side-effects.

Rodin draws our attention to the need for carefully scrutinizing the impacts on noncombatants, even if harm is unintended. He says:

> The increasing tendency to target "dual use" facilities such as power stations, transport, and media infrastructure is particularly worrying in this context, for destroying such targets has the potential to cause very significant noncombatant deaths for months and even years after the conflict has ended. If the war against terrorism is to avoid being a terrorist war, then such practices must be seriously reconsidered. (Rodin 2004:771)

The side-effects of otherwise legitimate military action may descend into transforming a just war into a terrorist war if reasonable care is not maintained. For Rodin, many of us have not been sensitive enough to this factor – which all of us wanting to combat terrorism should attend to.

Can we justify terrorism?

So, can terrorism ever be justified? Saul Smilansky (2004) claims that most of what is labelled "terrorism" is not justifiable.[3] He begins with two preliminary observations. First, he accepts the principle of noncombatant immunity. This is a prohibition on terrorism (and counterterrorism) activities severely harming or killing noncombatants. Second, Smilansky accepts what he describes as the anti-oppression exception to this principle. This exception would allow for targeting noncombatants "if it is necessary in combatting oppressive regimes" (Smilansky 2004:791).

Smilansky (2004:792) – who has a fine eye for paradoxes – surveys examples of terrorist activity finding "we have abundant terrorism without justification and possibly-justified terrorism that does not materialize."[4] After dismissing activities by organizations Such as Al-Qaeda as unjustified terrorism, he briefly considers possible areas where it might have been justified, such as in areas of extreme deprivation and severe poverty, but no such terrorist activity has taken place.

---

[3] See *The Global Justice Reader*, chapter 33.
[4] On paradoxes, see Smilansky (2007).

What to make of this? Smilansky draws our attention to what he describes as *illusions* of the practice of terrorism and its moral justification. He argues there is a phenomena of "justification bypassing" where the main issues are not some substantive moral concern like collective self-determination, basic cultural rights or the pursuit of personal freedom behind most terrorist activities, but rather "the ghosts of history, the depths of ill will and the temptations of power" that motivate much terrorism (Smilansky 2004:799). He adds:

> Fanatical religious and nationalistic pride and intolerance, the psychological attractions of being a "victim" rather than assuming responsibility for one's difficulties, an uncritical culture of resentment and envy, romantic idealizations of struggle and violence, open hatred of the other for its otherness, irrational myths, the self-destructive desire for mastery, and other such beliefs and passions seem to lie behind contemporary terrorism. (Smilansky 2004:799)

The key point is that, in principle, terrorism *might* be justifiable, but the terrorist organizations in operation around the world act contrary to this.

This leads Smilansky to strongly urge caution in being careful about permitting terrorism at all. He says: "we should err on the side of not allowing terrorism" as the risks of doing so – and the likelihood any terrorist activities will fall far short of being justified – are high (Smilansky 2004:800). Rather than acknowledging in practice the theoretical possibility of justified terrorism, we should not permit the practice whether or not it could be justified.[5]

Assassination and targeted killings

Let us explore further this connection between crimes and terrorism by examining *assassination*, which has been called "murder by treachery" (Gross 2003:351). Michael L. Gross (2003:351) says:

> First, international norms governing law enforcement carefully regulate the use of lethal force and leave no room for assassination, execution or targeted killings by law enforcement officials. Second, the law of armed conflict, while allowing ample room for lethal force, nevertheless proscribes assassination as a form of "perfidious" warfare. Assassination,

---

[5] For a debate over how terrorism might be justified and critical doubts, see Held (2008) and Brooks (2010).

often facilitated by local collaborators and informers, threatens the conventions of warfare and undermines the integrity of the civilian community. For this reason, the costs and benefits of assassination are grossly unbalanced.

These are significant reasons for why there should be a blanket ban on assassinations. Moreover, assassination is not law enforcement. If targets are criminals, then the methods used should be limited to infiltration, intelligence, arrest, and imprisonment. And if deemed an "armed combatant," a state risks being required to grand terrorists the legitimacy and protection afforded by the Geneva Convention (Gross 2003:351).

And, of course, there are limits on how far a state may go in self-defense. Assassinating opponents is widely thought to cross this line for the reasons stated above. Gross notes the perhaps surprisingly overlooked issue of mutual trust in war.[6] He says: "War, if we go by the standards of international law, is not a fight to the death. Rather, sides fight until they have disabled one another and forced the other side to surrender. Surrender is the key here" (Gross 2010:110). Soldiers need to trust that in waving a white flag in surrendering that they will be captured, but not killed. And soldiers receiving new captives must trust that the offer to surrender is not being used as an opportunity to kill them with a suicide vest. The problem with assassination, amongst the others, is that it violates trust in a similar way – and it could lead to "increase the suffering in war and make peace all the more difficult" (Gross 2010:110–111).

Assassinations today are more likely to happen through *targeted killing*, such as a drone strike, than poisoning although both continue to happen. Targeted killings are where a state engaged in "compiling lists of certain individuals who pose specific threats and then killing them when the opportunity presents itself" (Gross 2010:103). Typically, these killings happen against a backdrop of *asymmetric war* where military capabilities are so unequal that the two sides cannot make the same kinds of military attacks on the other – like one country striking another from afar using drones without any possibility of retaliation.

Gross considers how assassinating through targeted killings might be justified. The first condition is that it must be a means of last resort with other options exhausted. The method must be "unavoidable … to prevent an immediate ad grave threat to human life" (Gross 2010:106). These are generally the same conditions that would apply to law enforcement more generally.

---

[6] On the importance of trust in politics generally, see Brooks (2022c).

While difficult sometimes to know in practice, it is easy to conjure up a thought experiment – such as *the Sniper Stop Case*. Imagine there is a large army amassed on your country's border. The army is led by a dictator who has instructed his army to invade imminently. Both sides know the army is militarily superior and will win any conventional battle. But at this moment, your country has a sniper who could kill the dictator and prevent an invasion. In such a scenario, using the sniper to stop the war will lead to beneficial consequences, not least the saving of many lives.[7] But such circumstances rarely arise and difficult to discern if, or when, they do.

A second condition is that the target must be a combatant and never a noncombatant. Gross (2010:106) argues: "Ordinary combatants, if that is what they are, may be shot and killed solely for facing their enemy in wartime … Combatants are vulnerable regardless of the immediate threat they pose." A related, third condition is that any such action must happen when at war, not in peacetime. These conditions take some of the exceptionality out of assassination as, in conflict, active combatants can be targets for killing.

Fourth, we must have confidence in the effectiveness of the assassination. We require a high degree of certainty that the killing will achieve a desired effect and "leave little chance that the mission itself and/or subsequent retaliation would take more lives than the assassination saves" (Gross 2003:364; see 2010:119). Of course, an issue here is that no one has perfect knowledge about the future, not least any unforeseen (as they are by definition "unforeseen") consequences of one's actions. The high degree of certainty called for by Gross really must approach a cast-iron guarantee – as the risks of hugely negative consequences are at least as high at this.

Fifth, and finally, assassination must be rare. It must be an exception to the norm and not a rule. However, this raises the issue of the following: if there are several instances that satisfy all other conditions for justifying assassinations, why should they not all happen? How do we determine which are selected and which are not? Indeed, if there are many cases of imminent danger that can only be handled by targeted killings (as implausible as this might be in reality), then, at least in principle, these ought to be cases we act upon if we are willing to back this practice. So one issue is it is not clear what it means to ensure the practice is only exceptional. Furthermore, if we ought generally not to do it notwithstanding the several caveated conditions required for justification, this might seem a strong reason to not do so.

---

[7] For a view on how we might save the greatest number in a non-consequentialist way, see Brooks (2002b).

Terrorists use violence in ways meant to spread fear and create havoc. It is a form of violence that can take unconventional forms and target civilians in their everyday lives. Conventional military means are often inapplicable and the high stakes involved may make some support tougher measures than law enforcement. While concerns have been noted about the proposals, Gross (2003, 2010) offers a thought-provoking defense of controversial practices that should make us reflect more on the ways and means available to a society in tackling terrorists in their midst.

Conclusion

Terrorism is a significant concern in our modern world. Our lives are built on a trust of each other – which terrorist acts seek to shatter. This chapter has surveyed terrorism's definition, possible justification and the use of assassination and targeted killings. If we asked colleagues if they knew what terrorism is, we would expect them to answer in the affirmative. And yet, for a phenomena that it could be said "everybody knows," there are various differences in how leading scholars who define and pin the concept down. As we have seen, some would note the importance of targeting civilian noncombatants whereas others would include non-active duty combatants and others. Or some would see the state as a possible agent of terrorism whereas others would rule it out. But what they all have in common is the essence of causing terror through a threat of violence or actual violence to achieve some aim.

A key part of this is the terror must be deliberate. This might lead some to claim that actions aimed at targeting legitimate targets like active combatants could not be considered terrorist, even if they resulted in civilian deaths as a side-effect and create fear. This flows from the doctrine of double effect where the main aim intended is the military target and any side-effect is permissible. However, as we have seen, this doctrine is inapplicable where our targeting lacks a reasonable standard of care and is negligent or reckless. Even if our military actions are intended not to cause harm or fear to civilians, they would be unjustified.

We sadly have no shortage of examples of terrorist organizations in the world. We have explored the issue of, if terrorism could be justified, whether any of these organizations and their activities could meet this test. As we have seen, it has been argued that they all fall short – raising the intriguing puzzle that terrorist organizations that could be justified are not and possible groups that might in justified terrorism do not do so. This is meant to make us resist any urge to permit terrorism, which might in theory be justified, because of the high risks that are in practice, it will almost certainly fall short.

Finally, assassination and the use of targeted killing is sometimes put forward as an appropriate method for tackling terrorism. We considered the alleged benefits and costs of permitting such a policy. We have seen that some claim there might be a fairly narrow and rarely used justification for such practices, but also raised concerns that crossing this line might bring.

Together, the work surveyed challenges us about what terrorism is, what it aims to do, what targets it might have and how, if ever, it can achieve its ends. At a time where national security is under constant pressure, the need to understand terrorism and the ethics behind responding to it have never been greater.

Discussion questions

1. What is terrorism? Is it war by other means?
2. Can terrorism achieve its aims more reliably than other means?
3. Must terrorism intend to target civilians?
4. Is terrorism ever justifiable?
5. Is assassination or targeted killing ever justified?

10

Women and Global Justice

Introduction

This book has considered issues relating to justice in a monist way thus far. Some topics have been discussed in terms of the general duties applying to all individuals at all times. Others have centered on the special associative duties that apply to members of a group. We have thought about individuals as part of a humanity or a subset as, say, a national group. But while we have considered differences of place and culture, we have not yet examined differences of sex and gender – such as ideas about women and global justice – and this is addressed in this chapter.[1]

The contributions of women to the field of global justice have been enormous and wide-ranging. Some of these have been discussed in previous chapters (and it is important that they were).[2] We gain penetrating insights about perspective and particularity – of how shared institutions, national and global, do not impact nor work with all individuals equally in the same universal ways.

---

[1] For an excellent survey of work by women in global gender justice, see Jaggar (2020).

[2] While I believe issues about women and global justice as a distinct topic are an invaluable area to explore in its own right, I strongly oppose what I would call the *ghettoization* of feminist thought to only chapters on feminism. It is crucial that this work enters the mainstream and "normalized" taking its rightful place within our wider canon.

Global Justice: An Introduction, First Edition. Thom Brooks.
© 2023 John Wiley & Sons Ltd. Published 2023 by John Wiley & Sons Ltd.

In this chapter, we will examine the issue of how multiculturalism might impact women differently than men. We explore this debate between feminism and multiculturalism further in specifically considering whether polygamy can be acceptable and, if so, how as an example that helps distinguish the two main groups of feminism – liberal feminism and radical feminism. Finally, we will delve into the differing impact of global poverty on women and the debate in this area. While no chapter in any general introduction can cover every topic or contributor, these topics and issues represent some of the important works happening relating to women and global justice.

Is multiculturalism bad for women?

Susan Moller Okin's (1999) essay "Is Multiculturalism Bad for Women?" is one of the most cited in philosophy.[3] When we consider the piece, it is easy to see why. In much everyday talk, we might think about efforts to accommodate multiculturalism and its on the community *as a whole*. What is so useful in Okin's work – even if we disagree with her conclusions – is that she makes fundamentally clear that accommodating some aspects of multiculturalism has a disproportionate impact on women than men. This unequal impact matters.

Okin begins by noting how a growing number of Western countries were shifting their position from assimilation to accommodation. This move is driven by the view that to force individuals with a different culture to adopt the culture of their new adopted culture is oppressive (Okin 1999:9). In general, we may see the pursuit of multiculturalism and of feminism as "good things which are easily reconciled" (Okin 1999:10).

She next turns to definitions. Okin (1999:10) defines "feminism" as "the belief that women should not disadvantaged by their sex, that they should be recognized as having human dignity equal to that of men, and they should have the opportunity to live as fulfilling and as freely chosen lives as men can." Okin's feminism is *liberal feminism*. It puts a priority on women having equal individual rights to men and the importance of consent.

Okin (1999:11) defines "multiculturalism" as the view that "minority cultures or ways of life are not sufficiently protected by the practice of ensuring the individual rights of their members, and as a consequence these should also be protected through special *group* rights or privileges."[4]

---

[3] See *The Global Justice Reader*, chapter 34.
[4] Emphasis given.

She points out that multiculturalism supports cultural rights that can be exercised only by members of that culture. For example, the right to get married through a particular religious organization is available to its members, but they may and do exclude non-members from doing so. Or, as Okin (1999:11) notes, a right in France to have a polygamous marriage, but only for members of the relevant cultural group – and not available to all other citizens. Cultural rights are rights held only by members of that culture. And because, as she notes, culture is such a pervasive feature in our lives, demand for such rights is growing.[5]

Different views about group rights are noted. For example, some might say a liberal society should tolerate breaches of individual rights if it is a way of protecting that group's continued existence. They should be left alone and tolerated. But Okin (1999:11) strongly challenges this view as a fundamental breach of liberal views, such as "the moral equality of men and women" threatened by permitting illiberal cultural practices that might flout individual rights.

Okin (1999:12) rightly notes that not only is there unequal power between a minority group and the majority culture, but there is the unequal power between men and women that is "suffused" through all cultures (see Jaggar 2020:338). Equal opportunities are not secured for women and girls in relation to men and boys. Any society – including, but not limited to, minority groups – is "gendered, with substantial differences in power and advantage between men and women" (Okin 1999:12). Her argument is not to single out any minority cultural group. She is clear that *all* cultural groups – of East and West or North and South – have seen women treated unequally to men. Okin's critique of multiculturalism is a critique of all cultures and not a favoring of one over others.

In an especially insightful remark, Okin (1999:13) argues that cultural rights are not equal rights for women. Instead, the acceptance of special cultural rights is likely to widen the power imbalance more between women and men – and objectionable for that reason. When we think about some multicultural issues are about – such as, the laws of marriage (including forced marriage), female genital cutting, divorce, child custody, division and control of property, inheritance, and the wearing of headscarves, or other coverings – these "cultural practices" are likely to have a greater impact on women than men. She says: "home is, after all, where much of

---

[5] See Gould (2004:139–155) for an insightful analysis of human rights and women's rights. This article is included in only the first edition of *The Global Justice Reader*, chapter 36.

culture is practiced, preserved and transmitted to the young ... The more a culture requires or expects of women in the domestic sphere, the less opportunity they have of achieving equality with men in *either* sphere" (Okin 1999:13).[6] Multiculturalism is in these cases about expanding gender inequality in terms of unequal rights and unequal opportunities. Any liberal should take the side of rights and fair equality of opportunity instead – and, most especially, liberal feminists – and resist instances where "culturally based customs aim to control women" (Okin 1999:16).

In the long struggle for gender equality, cultural group rights might be seen as far more of a problem than a solution. In fact, Okin (1999:22) says some women may be better off if their culture became extinct and given no protection. But we *could* accommodate some cultural rights in theory, but *only* if these do not undermine individual rights and equal opportunities between women and girls. Moreover, any such decision *must* include the voices of women and girls. Again, as a liberal, Okin prioritizes individual rights and the importance of consent. The problem with cultural rights is these may undermine these rights, increase gender inequality and in a non-consensual way.

Okin's essay is one of the most cited – and discussed – in philosophy attracting much comment and critique. In the rest of this chapter, we will examine the issues she raises further with regards to how her views might be applied in the next section. The final section will consider culture, gender justice, and severe poverty.

Feminism and polygamy

Let us consider the issue of feminism and multiculturalism through an example. Okin (1999:9–11, 13, 15) repeatedly cites polygamy as an example of a cultural right that liberal feminists should oppose as a cultural practice. Her reason is that polygamy foments inequality between men and women. Today, polygamy almost exclusively takes the form of *polygyny* where one husband has two or more wives. *Polyandry* is much rarer where one wife has two or more husbands.[7] If polygamy were permitted, then this would legalize the more dominant form, polygyny – and so, as practiced, likely to provide a right for men to marry multiple wives, but not a right for women

---

[6] Emphasis added. On multiculturalism and equality, see Parekh on the "equality of difference" (2006:243–249).

[7] Polyandry tends to be practiced only in rural, sparsely populated areas such as Bhutan, Mongolia, and Tibet, for example.

to marry multiple husbands. This fits with Okin's concern that allowing cultural rights like polygamy would increase inequality between men and women while recognizing a right for men to exercise which women cannot use in the same way.

It is worth noting that, as Okin has claimed, cultural rights and gender inequality are not a worry for some cultures, but not others. Polygamy is neither exclusively Western or non-Western. Various cultural and religious groups have practiced it, including some Hindus, Mormons, Muslims, and others. This includes the Bible where several polygamous marriages are noted, beginning with Adam and Eve's grandson Lamech (the father of Noah) and other important biblical figures such as Abraham, David, and Solomon.[8] Polygamy would appear a fitting example of Okin's point that gender inequality runs through different cultures. It is therefore a concern for any liberal feminist as a structurally unequal practice that we should ban.

Other liberal feminists are sympathetic to the concern. For example, Martha C. Nussbaum (1999:98) recognizes that polygamy is "a structurally unequal practice." In her view, the most convincing argument against polygamy is that "men are permitted plural marriages, and women are not" (Nussbaum 2008:197). This is an asymmetry of power, rights and opportunity between men and women that is unjustified and unacceptable.

However, unlike Okin, Nussbaum does not argue that because polygamy is *practiced* in an unjustified way that it cannot be practiced *differently* in a justified way. Nussbaum claims her reservations are conditional.[9] If polygamy did not treat women unequally, then it could be supported. To break the asymmetrical treatment of men and women, women must share equal opportunities to marry more than one husband. Nussbaum (2008:197) says that "if there were a sex-equal polygamy" treating both the same and respected the consent of men and women to take part, then such a polygamy would be justified.

A similar argument is made by Cheshire Calhoun. Like Nussbaum, she does not believe that the unequal status of women in polygamy is essential to the practice of polygamy. She accepts that if the only form of polygamy used is polygyny, then the practice would be unacceptable. But it is not necessary that polygamy is only practiced in this one form. If we ensured polyandry was as available as polygyny, then women would not have an unequal status and polygamy can be justified (Calhoun 2005:1038–1040).

---

[8] See Genesis 4:15, 23, 25:1–2; 1 Samuel 25:43–44 and 1 Kings 7:8.

[9] See Nussbaum (2000:229–230) for views on polygamy in India. This chapter is included in only the first edition of *The Global Justice Reader*, chapter 35.

We can now see the debate among liberal feminists about polygamy. On the one side, we have Okin who argues that polygamy should be banned because the practice treats women unequally because it is practiced most often as polygyny. On the other side, we have Nussbaum and Calhoun who claim that polygamy is not essentially inegalitarian as we should ensure equal opportunities for polyandry, too. For the latter, liberal feminists are focused on equal individual rights and consent. Okin may be right to say that how we find polygamy is often objectionable, on this view, but polygamy is not essentially objectionable if practiced differently. Liberal feminists can support polygamy, if men and women had equal opportunities for polygynous or polyandrous marriages. This point is emphasized by Parekh (2006:286) who says: "Polygamy is not easy to dismiss for it does not violate any of the great universal or even the operative public values of liberal society." In principle, individuals could consent to the practice and have equal opportunities for each kind of polygamy.

Whereas liberal feminism believes that polygamy is not an essentially problematic practice for women if equal rights and consent obtain, a different view is *radical feminism* that finds polygamy an essentially problematic practice structurally.[10] For example, Thom Brooks (2009) argues that polygamy is a structurally unequal practice that discriminates against nonheterosexuals. He begins noting that polygamy is almost exclusively practiced as polygyny, where one man has two or more wives. Brooks (2009:116) claims that polygamy threatens the equality of men and women – and also the equality among polygamous partners. He draws attention to the asymmetrical ability to leave the marriage. While a husband can divorce any (or all) spouse(s), a wife can only divorce him.

The relationship is asymmetrical because only the husband can choose who will join or leave the relationship through either marriage or divorce. In contrast, his wives can only choose to marry or divorce their husband,

---

[10] Other examples include prostitution where some *liberal feminists* argue that, which many practices are objectionable, it is possible, with reform and safeguards, to justify a right to consent and participate whereas *radical feminists* claim such consent has limits and the practice of prostitution is structurally one of unequal power that should give us cause to reject it. While liberal and radical feminism are two important strands of feminist philosophy, there are not the only varieties. For a general introduction, see McAfee (2018).

but do not choose who else might join or leave the polygamous marriage. Brooks (2009:116) explains:

> Let us suppose that a husband has three wives: A, B and C. While each wife may have consented to each person entering into a polygamous marriage with a shared husband, this is where her consent ends. Each wife may only either agree to all polygamous partners or divorce her husband and leave behind his other wives. Instead, only the husband alone may agree to marry or divorce each wife. As a result, the husband may choose to divorce wife A or rather both wives B and C.

Polygamy is structured in a hub and spoke model. The individual at the center of the polygamous family agrees with each wife whether to join or leave the family. But the wives do not agree with each other whether to join or leave as well. As Calhoun (2005:1040) argues, polygamy would be acceptable if we could "assign equal importance to the consent to all spouses" including "the exit option of divorce to all spouses," then polygamy remains unjustified as spouses lack equal options to divorce. So, even if polygamy was equally available to men and women – with the same opportunities to form a polygynous or polyandrous marriage – individuals are treated unequally in polygamy's general hub–and–spoke model with the hub having more opportunity to exercise consent to members joining or leaving than the other spouses.

Brooks (2009:116–117) argues that polygamy might also discriminate against non-heterosexuals. Polygamy takes the form of either polygyny or polyandry. Both are heterosexual relationships that exclude nonheterosexuals.

A possible way to resolve these issues might be twofold. First, we might create some new version of plural marriage that is inclusive of nonheterosexuals to address this issue. However, there would remain a problem of the structural inequality of members with one another, given polygamy's inegalitarian structure and asymmetrical power. A second way is to consider *polyamory*, a relationship of three or more people that may have multiple men and/or women inclusive of any sexual orientation. As it lacks any set structure, there is greater possibility for equality between polyamorous relationship members. However, it would be conditional on whether or not, in fact, polyamorous relationships are, in practice, more equal.

Polygamy is presented as an example of what liberal feminists should reject on account of its treating men and women equally, according to Okin. However, other liberal feminists, like Nussbaum and Calhoun, rightly point out that liberals *could* accept polygamy under certain conditions, such as if equal opportunities and rights with the ability to consent are satisfied. In contrast, radical feminists, like Brooks, claim that these conditions cannot overcome the inegalitarian structure that is intrinsic to polygamy. This example shows how feminism is not one view or position. It is several. And different kinds of feminism gravitate towards different answers to philosophical questions. But what they have in common is a focus on inequalities between men and women and how these are best addressed – albeit in a variety of ways.

Culture, gender justice, and severe poverty

Severe poverty is a human problem, but it can impact women most. Women are disproportionately among the poorest of the world's population. As we saw in Chapter 7, various theories about global poverty take a monistic approach treating those in need as a single group. This raises the question about how best to address the different experiences – and difficulties – faced by women.

Susan Moller Okin (2003:281) notes that global poverty affects one in four human beings.[11] Of these approximately 1.3 billion (at that time and, tragically, growing), this has impacted women and girls most. Okin (2003:284) says:

> In many cultures, when any scarcity exists women and girls tend to get less to eat and less health care than men and boys in the same household; these disparities, in addition to sex-selective abortion and the neglect of widows, help to explain why, as Amartya Sen has dramatically phrased it, "more than a hundred million women are missing," mainly in South Asia and the PRC.[12]

Additionally, Okin notes that women and girls can often struggle with two or even three roles from traditional household chores, paid work and community organizing. Moreover, on average, mothers contribute more to their children from their available resources than do fathers. She claims that while virtually all of disadvantaged women's income is spent on the family's basic needs, poor men are more likely "to retain a

---

[11] See *The Global Justice Reader*, chapter 35.
[12] The "PRC" refers to the "People's Republic of China." The quote of Amartya Sen is from Sen (1990).

significant part of their income for their own personal use, such as smoking, drinking, gambling, and spending on other women" (Okin 2003:305). Unsurprisingly, when mothers are deprived of their income, time, energy, health or ability to provide essential care, "her deprivation affects her children far more than if their father were similar deprived" (Okin 2003:285).

All this points to the fact that a presumably "neutral" approach to poverty alleviation and development policy can impact men and women very differently, with further impact on children. In particular, resource-related approaches tend to measure economic value in terms of what is bought and sold in the economy. However, much of the work by women – and a very disproportionate share – is unpaid, from child care to domestic labor, women's hard work is often left out of the analysis (Okin 2003:286). Development models that focus only on GDP turn supportive efforts more to the work of men than that of many women (Okin 2003:287).

Okin (2003:295, 301–302) argues that a particular problem is that women's voices are not being heard and absent from policy decision-making. If they were listened to, then we would all hear is:

> What the people say they lack, overwhelmingly, are assets and resources that could enable them to cope, by working, to make a reliable living for themselves. Well-being is having the ability to feed, clothe, and shelter themselves and their children, as well to provide them with the health care and education necessary for their avoiding poverty in the future. (Okin 2003:306)

And they would want some control to overcome their vulnerabilities:

> On top of anxiety about meeting their basic material needs, they suffer from the lack of voice, power, and independence. They speak repeatedly of not being listened to or of having no influence on or control over events around them of the humiliation of being exposed to exploitation and to rude and inhumane treatment, of being harassed, of being without necessary documents because they lack connections, knowledge, or the ability to pay bribes, of being beholden to others for fulfilment of their daily needs. (Okin 2003:307)

For Okin, these everyday concerns of women living in severe poverty tell a vivid story. It is a narrative of inequality, vulnerability, and unfairness which helps expose how modern development approaches fail to capture the full reality with a one-size-fits-all approach, especially missing the lived reality of women who urgently require extra support. They have a stake in society and they wish, and deserve, a say in its planning.[13]

In response to Okin's essay, Martha C. Nussbaum (2004:193) begins by stating her agreement with the view that there is an urgent need to have approaches addressing the needs of the world's poor that particularly focus on the needs of women in these communities.[14] But Nussbaum takes issue with Okin's critique of her capabilities approach as insufficiently responsive to women's voices.

Nussbaum (2004:197) argues that her argument for capabilities – discussed in Chapter 7 – is able to take in account reasonable pluralism in the world.[15] She notes that her list of 10 capabilities is purposively drafted in an abstract and general way. This is to allow room for citizens and their governments to deliberate about these capabilities so their implementation is appropriate for their community. This is because "different nation should do this somewhat differently, taking their histories and special circumstances into account" (Nussbaum 2004:198).

Nussbaum (2004:198) claims that her capabilities list can be endorsed by people who otherwise have very different views of the good. It is a universal framework that can be usefully applied to particular communities in a way that best fits their particularity without changing standards for justice from one community to the next. Capabilities are a conception of justice from the ground up. As Nussbaum (2004:1999) says, "it will only be implemented if the voices of those involved actually sign on to it." Her analysis focused on India so as not to dilute a deep, concrete application of her views in a particular setting with broader, more removed-from-everyday-life that might occur if doing some global survey (Nussbaum 2004:201).

To some degree, Okin and Nussbaum debate the issue of who, if anyone, can speak for the voices of others and its impact on our theories of justice. Nussbaum (2004:205) claims:

But the result can ultimately only be judged by each reader, reading Socratically.[16] By using detailed examples that convey the nature and complexity of the issues faced by the Indian women's movement, and by surrounding them with references to a wide range of scholarly works

[13] On stakeholding and justice, see Brooks (2016c, 2021).

[14] See *The Global Justice Reader*, chapter 36.

[15] See Nussbaum (2003) on capabilities as fundamental entitlements. This chapter is included in only the first edition of *The Global Justice Reader*, chapter 34.

[16] For one view on what the Socratic method is, see: https://www.law.uchicago.edu/socratic-method.

and a wide variety of organizations, I hope I have provided materials that readers can consult independently, in order to validate or contest my claims.

If we do not come from a similarly lived experience as those struggling in severe poverty, it may be difficult – and contested – to discern and explain in our way what this experience is like, what its most significant challenges are, and what are the possible future solutions.[17] However, Nussbaum is surely correct that, from whatever our vantage point, the best that we can do is simply *to make best sense* of it – and to "validate or contest" claims in light of it. There may be no one correct answer or we may find that as our understanding deepens and changes, so too our views on the best response. These speak to the limitations of our experience and first-hand knowledge, but – like a ship at sea – through continued engagement with the voices of those impacted we can develop a more compelling view for ourselves and others.

Conclusion

Global justice can often be discussed as a kind of *universal* justice. The duties and responsibilities we have to an individual in severe poverty might be thought to relate to all others in the same way. In this chapter, we have surveyed some leading contributions to how we might think about the different lived experiences of women and the implications for global justice.

Each topic challenges conventional ideas we might have about how justice should be applied. First, we might think that feminism and multiculturalism are both projects that we should pursue in a more tolerant society. We have considered arguments by Okin that this should be opposed because many of the cultural rights, if permitted, would make inequalities between men and women worse. So, the issue is not about whether we should be making an exception for a group to show respect, but rather whether it is ever acceptable to allow any group's cultural rights to trump individual rights.

Second, we considered the specific case of polygamy. There is little disagreement that polygamy as currently practiced is objectionable. The issue is whether feminism might justify the practice and, if so, how. We have seen that some liberal feminists claim it is possible to support a reformed view of polygamy with safeguards in place to ensure men and women have equal

---

[17] See Jaggar (2005, 2020) for important health warnings with this approach and see Watene (2020) on what can learned from listening to indigenous philosophies.

opportunities to forge a polygamous relationship and consent. If so, this view of feminism could support it. In contrast, we have also seem the view of radical feminism that claims polygamy is, by structure, an inherently inegalitarian practice that cannot respect equal rights, even if someone wanted to consent to the relationship. This case highlights some of the diversity in feminist thought and how different views can support different positions.

Third, and finally, we examined lessons to be learned from listening to women's voices. For some, like Okin, this exercise is necessary and urgent to highlight the need for sympathetic empathy and understanding at a concrete, practical level. For others, like Nussbaum, they agree on the necessity and urgency, but believe it is possible to draw out general and abstract principles with universal applicability. This debate again shows the diversity in feminist thought.

Global justice is not one thing. It impacts communities differently and women disproportionately. Thinking about this impact on women is not tangential to global justice theorizing, but essential to it as this chapter has tried to demonstrate.

Discussion questions

1. Is multiculturalism bad for women?
2. How should we balance group rights and women's rights?
3. Is polygamy a problem?
4. Does severe poverty impact men and women in different ways? If so, how?
5. How can theories of global justice best relate to the issues raised by women in severe poverty? Does it improve our theories?

11

Climate Change

Introduction

Our world is changing. One of our greatest challenges is taking action on climate change.[1] What is happening is significant. Roughly ten percent of the Earth's land is covered by ice sheets or glaciers. These are melting because the surface air temperature in areas like the Arctic has more than doubled the global average for two decades with the Antarctic's ice sheet ice sheet over the last decade, too IPCC (2019:6).

This has unlocked frozen moisture contributing to two problems. First, it causes raising sea levels that threaten coastal communities and risk sinking small island countries like Tuvalu. Since 1902, the sea has risen about six inches; but, by 2100, the level is expected to rise between 1.3 and 2.6 ft (Royal Society 2020). This had led to *environmental refugees* as people seek safety in light of a climate emergency (Risse 2009). Second, the unfrozen, extra moisture circulating in the atmosphere has led to an increasing frequency of extreme weather events (IPCC 2014:4). This contributes to heavier rainfalls, more dangerous hurricanes and a shifting jet stream with changing weather patterns. As these shifts happen, they impact the

---

[1] Presented as the issue of "international environmental justice" in the first edition of *The Global Justice Reader*, Part XI.

Global Justice: An Introduction, First Edition. Thom Brooks.

environment with a greater likelihood of droughts, an increase in wildfires and spread tropical diseases to new geographical areas.

And this is all before considering increasing pollution of our air, land and seas. The United Nations Environmental Program estimates that for every square mile of ocean there are roughly 46000 pieces of plastic in it. Acid rain, smog, poor sanitation and more are now a part of everyday life for billions of people.

There is no doubting the cause of the problem. It's us. The United Nation's Intergovernmental Panel on Climate Change (IPCC 2019)'s reports make clear that the fact of climate change is unequivocal and its primary cause is human activity. The damage done is difficult to undo. If all carbon emissions were reduced to zero instantly, there is already enough carbon emissions to continue global warming for decades (IPCC 2020). The only real disagreement among scientists is not whether there is climate change or whether humans are to blame for it, but over predictions of how bad – and there is no doubt it will be bad on current trajectories – things will get (Mastrandrea and Schneider 2010:8). So, what to do?

This chapter will survey the main sides in this debate. First, it will consider views of mitigation aimed at conservation. These ideas include models for limiting each state's emissions and making polluters pay to address the harms they create. Secondly, we will examine views of adaptation. Climate change is already happening. Adaptation proponents argue we should prioritize adapting ourselves to climate change in future. Each side claims to offer a solution, but this is challenged in the final section. It will be argued that climate change can be exacerbated by human conduct, but not stopped permanently and environmental catastrophes have happened before there were any human beings. This view pushes us to see sustainability in a light – and the challenge of addressing climate change as even more daunting.

Tragedy of the commons

Climate change has been described as "a perfect moral storm" (Gardiner 2011:22). There is no doubt that human activity is reasonable for the climate change we see today. However, "the impact of any particular emission of greenhouse gases is not realized solely at its source, either individual or geographical; instead, impacts are dispersed to other actors and regions of the earth" (Gardiner 2011:24). This makes it difficult to pinpoint where to apportion blame for the impact from vast numbers of individuals and institutions creating emissions.

Stephen Gardiner (2002) likens this moral storm about climate change to *the tragedy of the commons*.[2] The tragedy was first argued for by Garrett Hardin (1968, 1974). In essence, the tragedy is that the rapid growth of the human population, if left unabated, risks serious problems for future generations and the environment.

Hardin imagines a group of farmers grazing their cattle on common land that is shared. Each farmer is keen to gain the most he can. If he adds an additional animal, he gains the full benefits from selling it. But if the commons are overgrazed, he shares a fraction of the total loss with the other farmers. Hardin (1968:1244) argues:

> The rational herdsman concludes that the only sensible course for him to pursue is to add another animal to his herd. And another ... But this is the conclusion reach by each and every rational herdsman sharing a commons. Therein lies the tragedy. Each man is locked into a system that compels him to increase his herd without limits – in a world that is limited. Ruin is the destination toward which all men rush, each pursuing his own best interests in a society that believes in the freedom of the commons. Freedom in a commons brings ruing to all.

The tragedy of the commons is that what is rational for each individual separately, leads to a terrible result for all individuals collectively. Gardiner (2002:396) notes the relevance of Hardin's tragedy to human overpopulation is weakened by falling global fertility rates whereby global population growth is slowing.[3]

But Hardin's tragedy is a genuine threat (Gardiner 2011:27; see Brooks 2020a:25–26). We have a "commons" in our land, sea, and air. In producing more emissions, I might benefit economically from increased production. However, our planet has but one atmosphere. Without some means of global control, individual pursuits will add up to international calamity – and for the next generation: we damage the environment in ways now – with carbon emissions remaining in the atmosphere for decades after they were produced – that will impact most future generations who are not here and who do not have a voice. And the full effects will not be seen or felt immediately as "human-induced climate change is a severely lagged phenomena" (Gardiner 2011:32). There will be a temptation for some for

---

[2] See *The Global Justice Reader*, chapter 37.

[3] Gardiner (2002:400) notes "Hardin's analysis of the population problem as a tragedy of the commons is fatally flawed," but his use of the tragedy model has application when thinking about environmental impact.

"buck-passing" (literally passing the buck to others) of this problem to future others (Gardiner 2011:36, 43).

This issue of *intergenerational justice* – of our duties today to individuals in future who may not yet exist – poses a significant challenge in moral motivation. This is because we must make sacrifices leaving us worse off than we might be otherwise *today* to avoid environmental catastrophe for others *in future*. What is more, global partial compliance is insufficient to avoid this worst outcome. Gardiner (2002:412) says: "without full cooperation one is at best delaying global warming, not arresting it." The significant concern – for all of us – is that our state and global institutions, as constituted currently, appear inadequate for this challenge (Gardiner 2011:28).

Mitigation

So, what to do about this problem? Political philosophers have offered several contributions to how the problem of climate change might be solved; or, in Gardiner's (2011:412) words to not simply be "at best *delaying* global warming, but *arresting* it" and so bringing climate change under control.[4]

Most philosophers argue we need to look for solutions that combine both mitigation and adaptation. *Mitigation* is about conserving our consumption and alleviating, where possible, the effects of climate change. *Adaptation* is concerned with using technologies to help us adjust to a planet with a changed climate. Where there is disagreement over which of these two overlapping approaches to emphasize. Let us first consider mitigation.

One of the most popular pro-mitigation proposals is the idea of the *ecological footprint*. Our footprint is a measure of our planet's human carrying capacity: the maximum amount of natural resource consumption that can be sustained indefinitely. Mathis Wackernagel and William E. Rees (1996:3) say:

> The Ecological Footprint concept is simple, yet potentially comprehensive ... It is about humanity's continuing dependence on nature and what we can do to secure Earth's capacity to support a humane existence for all in the future. Understanding our ecological constraints will make our sustainability strategies more effective and livable.

Our ecological footprint is calculated through dividing up the global ecosystem, incorporating land and sea as required, into an equal share – or

---

[4] Emphasis added.

"footprint" – for every individual (Wackernagel 2009). The ecological footprint "is a measure and not a space" creating equalized sized shares of a generic space within the Earth's ecosystem and not a carving up of any particular space (Brooks 2020a:17).

The purpose of the ecological footprint is it helps identify both how far countries may (or may not) exceed their footprint. We can assess each country by combining the footprints of their people. This approach makes clear that some countries are well beyond their proportionate equal share – and their *ecological debt* – and threaten global sustainability more than others.[5] For example, Peter Singer (2004:31) says

> The average Americans, by driving a car, eating a diet rich in the products of industrialized farming, keeping cool in summer and warm in winter, and consuming products at a hitherto unknown rate, uses more than fifteen times as much of the global atmospheric sink as the average Indian.[6]

In this illustration, Singer compares equal shares per person of the atmosphere's "sink" (e.g. its sustainable carrying capacity) similar in concept to the idea of a footprint. Through this common measure, we have a basis for making comparisons and a basis for action setting out the gaps we find between our equal shares and which countries go far beyond them which threaten the ecosystem we all enjoy – and rely on to survive.

It is worth noting two features about determining our fair shares that can change over time. The first feature is the size of the human population. If there are more people in future than now, then dividing up the ecosystem into equal shares will mean *smaller* shares for all. Likewise, if there are fewer people in future, our equal shares would increase. Global population size can make shares go up or down. A second feature is the ecosystem itself. If its sustainable carrying capacity decreased for some reason, then there is less to carve up for each individual – we would each get a *smaller* share if this happened even if no increase in the total population. But if the sustainable carrying capacity increased, then shares could get larger without the population shrinking as there would be more to equally carve out per person.

---

[5] Ecological debt is the unequal share of the ecosystem understood as unpaid debts from the wealthiest countries (which industrialized earliest through consumption-heavy processes) to developing counties (which have been most adversely impacted from the climate change arising from these consumption-heavy processes). See Simms (2009).

[6] This article is included in only the first edition of *The Global Justice Reader*, chapter 37.

The use of the footprint is often championed as a reliable measure that is fair and equitable, as it divides up the ecosystem the same, equal way for all. However, there are a few concerns expressed about its fairness and equality. First, it is unclear that insisting all are kept within the same footprint treats everyone equally (see Caney 2012:262). Energy needs are different at the beginning or end of life which may require greater resource needs. So, if we insisted on the same sized footprint for everyone, what might be comfortable for one person might be too little for another because they have different needs.[7]

In reply, it might be said that we should determine ecological footprints *not* as a specific individual's share, but as an *average* share over a life. But even so, people live in different climates. Different climates come with different resource needs. The four seasons in New England with humid summers and snowy winters are different to the dry heat of the Arizona sun. Or, put another way, there are different resource needs living in a cooler climate than in a rain forest. Ecological footprints are determined the same size for individuals, but may impact us differently – and some might argue unfairly – not because of what we want to do but because of the energy needs relative to our local climate. These differ and it might be argued that the system's inflexibility treats some less fair than others.

Secondly, insisting on an equal footprint may be unfair, too. Societies have developed differently in relation to their relative wealth and technological advancements. Thom Brooks (2020a:23) argues:

> An equal per capita footprint would ossify – and render more permanent – the relative global positions of the more affluent and technologically advanced countries in contrast to developing countries, which lack such infrastructure. The former would be in a much better position to make the most from their limited footprint. This would permit them to better retain their position of global privilege over less capable societies.

Affluent countries have a dominant position in global economy. Limiting ecological footprint shares after they have become postindustrial economies could cement their dominance over other countries that have much further to go in industrializing as they attempt to keep up. This is because the limiting shares will restrict the amount of ground that can be made up. Equal shares could engender unfairness – although it global economic

---

[7] I emphasize a difference in *needs*, but do not discuss differences in *wants* which might be more an issue of optional taste.

inequalities might be a price worth paying if it could secure a sustainable future, at least for some, but this would be a counterintuitive consequence of a fair and equal approach that could lead to unfairness and inequality.

A further issue raised by Simon Caney (2012:280–282) is that the ecological footprint approach is impractically siloed from other important and relevant factors.[8] He argues that, even if climate negotiators lacked the power to enforce the redistribution of other goods, they should take into account the distribution of other goods when making decisions (Caney 2012:282). For example, countries in severe poverty are often most impacted by the damaging effects of climate change. The former is relevant to the latter and *vice versa*. Climate change does not happen in isolation from other global problems and we should reflect on their interconnections.

A second mitigation approach is called the *polluter pays principle* (Caney 2005:752).[9] This principle is built off of the idea that we have a negative duty to compensate others for the harm that we have caused to them. Polluters should pay and compensate others for the damaging greenhouse gas emissions that polluters create. This compensation should minimize, if not annul, environmental damage by correcting damage caused and making polluting more costly leading to reduced emissions. In this way, a polluter pays principle pays for itself as an income-generating policy that helps us to mitigate – and conserve – the planet in a sustainable way.

The big questions for the principle are, namely, who should pay – and how much? Neither is answered easily. Let us consider each in turn.

It is not a straightforward issue to determine who should pay. This view is not held by everyone. For example, James Garvey (2008:115) says:

> It is a straightforward fact that some countries have emitted more greenhouse gases – used up more of the planet's sinks, caused more climate change – than others. It's a quantifiable fact: we know something about cumulative emissions.

This expresses a historical view about the polluter pays principle. It is an attractive perspective for those, like Garvey, who seek to ensure that polluters, as a whole, pay for all the pollution they create.

But there are several problems with this. First, data on cumulative emissions does not go back especially far – and the further back we go, the less confidence we have in the data. Second, it is unclear where to set the cutoff

---

[8] See *The Global Justice Reader*, chapter 38.
[9] This article is included in only the first edition of *The Global Justice Reader*, chapter 38.

point. Do we measure up from when we have reliable records, but leave out what we do not? This would allow countries that polluted before this arbitrary deadline to effectively get away without paying and leaving the full bill for others. Or do we look for a pleasant looking number like 25 or 50 years back? This still allows countries polluting before then to avoid paying their fair share.

Third, many of those who created carbon emissions are gone; they're dead. Our emissions can remain in the atmosphere for many decades. Not every polluter remains alive to pay. So, do we require the living to pay their share – plus pay for the emissions of past generations? Fourth, the behavior of past generations might have been different if they knew there would be something to pay. This raises an issue of fairness about whether people should be required to pay for emissions that, at that the time of creating them, there was no such requirement intended. It may strike some as taxing people for something they consumed – perhaps paying a tax for sugary foods – many years ago – is to create a duty where there had not been a corresponding responsibility and, thus, unfair.

Fifthly, there is an issue of compensating for climate damage. Suppose we could determine which polluters should pay and how much. Some environmental damage can be corrected: we can build flood defenses or create genetically modified crops. But some damage is of non-compensatory goods. For example, what should be paid out when countries sink below the sea level and are no more – or when species are made extinct? It is unclear how such problems could be addressed satisfactorily.

This has led some to argue instead for a *beneficiary*, not polluter, *pays principle* (Atkins 2018). The argument is that it is difficult, if not impossible, to identify all polluters who have contribution to emissions currently in our ecosystem, partly as some will have died but their emissions remain in the environment. But it is much easier to identify those who *benefit* from emissions as this will be current populations and measured against emission uses.

The principle is controversial for several reasons. First, it is difficult to get a satisfactory precision about the relative levels of benefit *from greenhouse gas emissions* for current societies. This is partly a by-product, as we have seen, with inexact data on emissions generally and the arbitrariness in choosing cut-offs for the time period (e.g. since when?) we would measure benefits from emissions. Secondly, it holds people today responsible for emissions they did not create, could not prevent, did not request, and took place in many cases before they were born.

There is also the following problem. We make a distinction between a *fee* and a *fine* (Sandel 2005:93–96). We pay fees to watch a sporting event or to join a club. However, we pay fines when we do wrong, such as when breaking the law (e.g. speeding or parking tickets) or not reporting our taxes on time. When we pay fines, these are for actions that we ought not perform – and there can be serious consequences for multiple breaches. For example, if you receive too many fines for driving, you risk having your driver license suspected or revoked. This raises the point that if the polluter pays principle is like a fine, it suggests that polluting ought not to happen, but it allows for us to pollute so long as we can pay for it. Thus, it seems to be essentially problematic.

Carbon emissions have been described as "the greatest market failure the world has ever seen" (Stern 2009:11). This is because the price of goods, including oil, does not reflect the true costs to society of their production and use. This is much more than putting gasoline in a car's tank, but includes the emissions of its extraction and the emissions produced to remain in the atmosphere for decades. Goods might need to reflect their full price – as someone must ultimately pick up the bill for addressing the consequences of its use. There is debate about how much this should be and often proposed that about US$2 extra per barrel of oil would suffice (Pogge 2002:205).

The polluter pays principle is popular with policy-makers for two primary reasons. First, it offers a clear rationale for raising new revenues. The principle aims to create income to assist governments in addressing environmental issues, such as tackling the effects of climate change. Getting polluters to pay some extra cost to go towards these efforts has been promoted as a reasonable price to pay.

Secondly, the principle's aim is to reduce emissions. The idea is that higher oil prices would lower demand. The polluter pays principle is not only about raising funds to tackle climate change's effects, but a means to influence behaviors to mitigate against further effects. A problem with this argument is that while it is correct that higher costs can lead to fewer emissions, there is no evidence that emissions could drop to anything sufficiently low as is required (Brooks 2020a:41). Indeed, we might call the principle the *polluters can pollute as much they can pay for principle*. In principle, if a polluter can pay the higher costs, then the polluter may pollute. The principle assumes lower use could become sustainably so with a relatively modest tax on oil. But this seems implausible given usage against fluctuations in price and the principle does not guarantee that emissions cannot exceed the Earth's carrying capacity.

Some polluter pays principle advocates are sensitive to these objections. For example, Caney (2005:769) argues that we are all under a duty to not exceed our quota for carbon emissions. Global emissions must be capped to ensure a sustainable future while the funds generated from the tax on emissions is used for mitigation efforts. In this way, Caney attempts to show how the principle can raise much needed revenue while not allowing emissions above an unsustainable level.

The problem with this is the principle loses its motivational force. The polluter pays principle is grounded on a negative duty to correct for harm caused. But if all emissions happen under a sustainable cap, there is then – in theory, anyway – no harm caused that requires correcting (and a principle to create the funds to do it). Instead of a duty in its own right, the polluter pays principle becomes another tax as a means of generating revenue, not a means of compensatory justice.

Adaptation

In addition to mitigation, a second approach to climate change is to focus on adaptation. Most argue that whatever we do must account for both mitigation and adaptation. This is because we are causing emissions beyond any sustainable level – and we must adapt to an already changing world. However, as with mitigation, there are some who argue on balance our primary focus should be on adaptation over mitigation. This section will survey some of these views.

The *adaptation* approach sees making changes to acclimatize ourselves is essential and not optional given the climate change we are seeing already. For example, global temperature is expected to rise by at least 1.5 °C this century – and quite possibly 2 °C or higher. The difference between 1.5 and 2 °C is the difference between whether 70% or 99% of coral reefs die and whether the Arctic Ocean is bare of any sea ice once per century or each decade and more frequently.[10] Either way, big changes are afoot and we will prepare for them (Gardiner 2004:573).

Adaptation measures can take a variety of forms, such as:

- Carbon dioxide removal, such as through reforestation or direct capture of carbon from the atmosphere
- Greater energy efficiency
- Improved home insulation
- Investment in public services reducing reliance on private transport
- Increased recycling
- Use of labelling and nudges to shift common behaviors
- Improved management of sewage and waste water

---

[10] See UN Environment Program (2020).

Some adaptative ideas include *substituting* just emissions for unjust emissions. For example, Caney (2012:286–289) argues we can lessen impact on the environment through greater energy efficiency, using non-carbon-based alternative energy sources, more ecologically-friendly agricultural, and construction practices. Where we can find new energy sources, we should use them – to do otherwise would do more harm than good (Caney 2012:291).

Other adaptative ideas include *geoengineering*. A well-known proposal is solar radiation management where airplanes are loaded with sulphate particles and spray them at 65 000 ft in several thousand flights annually. The aim would be to deflect solar radiation and create a cooling effect – mimicking the output of a volcanic eruption (Crutzen 2006). Additional ideas include relocating communities, flood defenses, and creating drought-resistant crops.

There are some possible objections to our overly relying on adaptation. First, there is significant uncertainty about the likely success of adaption measures. We cannot safely test many of the adaptative proposals put forward in anything like a controlled laboratory. There would be some degree of uncertainty with the risk of very high costs for failures. Unsurprisingly, most proposed measures have either not been tried or do not yet exist.

Much is placed on having a belief that things can only get better with future technology – we need only have faith, solutions will appear in time. For example, Matthew Kahn (2010:243) claims: "in a world with billions of educated, ambitious individuals, the best adaptations and innovations will be pretty good." Or "we will save ourselves by adapting to our ever-changing circumstances … At the end of the day, the story will have a happy ending" (Kahn 2010:7, 12).

Adaptation is viewed as a "cheap and simple" solution (Levitt and Dubner 2010:177). This leads some to claim there are it is more cost-effective to prioritize adaptation. For example, Bjørn Lomborg (1998:318) says: "it will be far more expensive to cut CO_2 emissions radically than to pay the costs of adaptation to the increased temperatures." Full mitigation is estimated to cost about two percent of GDP per annum (or roughly US$1 trillion annually) (Stern 2009:54). The argument is that partial mitigation is much cheaper. While it does not reduce emissions as far as possible, it is possible – it is claimed – to make up the difference in effect by a less costly investment in adaptation. The money saved could be used to better fund other major issues, like severe poverty alleviation (Lomborg 2008:8, 35; Posner and Weisbach 2010).

However, a word of caution is needed. We need to question the certainty on which these cost–benefit calculations are made. We need to know the effects of both mitigation efforts and likely untested or even undiscovered future technologies against – all in light of the risk our calculations might go wrong and we may damage the environment in ways that cannot be compensated nor corrected. Generally speaking, there is a much greater appetite for risk among adaptation proponents in comparison to those who prioritize mitigation.

Furthermore, as Dale Jamieson (2008:13) points out:

> Technological approaches are popular both with politicians and with the public because they promise solutions to environmental problems without forcing us to change our values, ways of life, or economic systems ... the image of the scientist as the "can-do" guy who can solve any problem remains quite potent.

Cheap solutions to major challenges that leave lives unchanged will be popular with most people at first glance. The issue is that what sounds too good to be true can be. No doubt, scientists have made extraordinary progress in how we use energy and impact the environment. But the effects can be surprisingly counterproductive in how significant technological advances with transformational potential can lead to unintended – and even unwanted – consequences. For example, Richard Wilkinson and Kate Pickett (2010:223) argue:

> More power-efficient washing machines or better insulated houses will help the environment, but they also cut our bills, and that immediately means we lose some of the environmental gain by spending the saved money on something else. As cars have become more fuel-efficient we have chosen to drive further. As houses have become better insulated we have raised standards of heating, and as we put in energy-saving light bulbs the chances are that we start to think it doesn't matter so much leaving them on.

The big advances made in energy efficiency has not led to expected emission reductions. If we were to rely on adaptation, we would need higher confidence both in what future technology could achieve – and in public support for achieving its potential – neither of which we likely have.

Rethinking sustainability

Mitigation and adaptation strategies are usually *both* a part of any proposed solution to the problem of climate change. It is widely accepted that reducing emissions and adapting to an already changing planet are necessary. Where there is disagreement is over which might have more priority and emphasis. But there is something else they both tend to agree on – and that is that they can provide a *solution* to the problems associated with climate change. We are told that "the world now has the technologies and financial resources to stabilize climate" (Brown 2011:198). We can ensure "a happy ending" if only we implement the right policy (Kahn 2010:12).

This is what I call an *end-state solution* (see Nozick 1974:153–155). It is the idea that, if we get our policies right, we can have a stable climate forever more. Significant changes to the environment or the risk of environmental catastrophe will no longer be possibilities. We can achieve an "end-state" of climate calm (Brooks 2016d:127–128; Brooks 2020d).

As Thom Brooks (2016d:127) argues, it is neither true that *only* human beings can impact climate change nor that, if *only* human beings did not impact the climate, it would not change.[11] The issue here is that the mainstream can be mistaken about the kind of problem that climate change represents. This point is also made by others:

In this world without us, traditional evolution would indeed revive, and the procession of geological ages would resume, though without anyone around to given them names (unless in the fullness of time a new creature, perhaps some gifted fish, evolves to the point at which it can assume the task) (Schell 2020:5).

Brooks (2016d:127–128; Brooks 2020a:64) notes that global environmental catastrophes do not require human beings to happen. There have been five catastrophes in our planet's past already. Events like ice ages, major volcanic eruptions, and meteors striking the Earth have been causing mass extinctions since millions of years before human beings first evolved, including the extinction of the dinosaurs.

We currently search for approaches that might best achieve what we can call *permanent sustainability*. This is when, if we stick with a set course of action, we can ensure a sustainable future without catastrophe. What we realize now is that this misunderstands the challenge. We cannot guarantee a catastrophe-free future.

Instead, we need to adopt a view of *impermanent sustainability* (Brooks 2020a:66). Whereas permanent sustainability looks to create a stable *status quo*, impermanent sustainability is a process of continual readjustment denying any fixed mode or formula to rely on. It reacts to a reality

---

[11] See *The Global Justice Reader*, chapter 39.

where we can never be comfortably settled, but continually challenging ourselves to reduce our impact on the climate while improving our adaptability.

Some might argue that, if catastrophe is always on the horizon in our endangered world, there is little, if anything, we might do about it since we cannot prevent it happening at some point in future. We do not know exactly when the next catastrophe might strike. But we do know it will happen more quickly and the tipping point more deadly and powerful if we do not act. Reducing impact and adjusting to constant change can help to delay the tipping point being reached buying us time to prepare as best we can while doing what we can to lessen its dangerous impact.

This way of thinking about climate change opens up a new climate change ethics. Brooks (2016d:128) says:

> we might approach climate change from a new perspective. our focus should not only be on how we might reduce our environmental impact, but we should extend our focus to another question: what are the normative implications of a future environmental catastrophe both foreseeable and perhaps inevitable? This different focus reinterprets climate change as a problem of management where we approach these questions in a new way. our proposals should reconsider sustainability for a tragic world—our tragic world—where the choices we have are less clear cut and more sobering than the overly, and unrealistically, optimistic solutions already offered.

An endangered world in the shadow of its next climate catastrophe demands more, not less, from us on this view. Climate change does not have some silver bullet that can put the problem to rest nor a happily ever after of sunny uplands. Instead, it requires greater efforts for an even larger challenge than many have recognized with no room for complacency.

Conclusion

Climate change is happening – and accelerating. This change threatens coastal communities, creates more intense and damaging extreme weather events, makes drought worse and helps tropical diseases to spread to new areas. These changes are found globally and requires a global response. However, it is an issue that requires making changes now that may make us worse off; but, if we do not, the situation will become even more bad for future generations.

This chapter has surveyed the main approaches to climate change. The first is mitigation approaches that aim at conservation. We considered the ecological footprint and polluter pays principles. Each offers different ways in which we can achieve a more sustainable future by securing reduced emissions. The second approach we considered is adaptation. This looks towards advances in science and technology to secure a more sustainable future.

We then critically reflected on what these two approaches share: namely, the view that, if enacted correctly, either might bring an end to climate change and create a sustainable forever after. This picture does not cohere with the scientific backdrop. Even if we had no impact – or if there were no human beings on Earth – this has not prevented environmental catastrophes from happening in our planet's past. We should reject the view that sustainability can become a permanent end-state of our future lives. Instead, we ought to embrace a view of impermanent sustainability that is sensitive to our having no one fixed way of being – other than doing our best to take any step we can to minimize our ecological impact and as much time as possible to develop the best adaptive technologies to prepare us as well as we can, for living in the shadow of a future climate catastrophe.

Discussion questions

1. What makes climate change a problem?
2. How can we mitigate climate change?
3. Can we apply a polluter pays principle?
4. Should we focus primarily on adapting to climate change?
5. What does impermanent sustainability look like?

Conclusion

Global justice matters. The issues it focuses on are some of the most important topics in political philosophy, such as sovereignty, rights to self-determination, human rights, nationalist and cosmopolitan theories of justice, immigration and citizenship, global poverty, just war theory, terrorism, women and global justice, and climate change. As "global" issues, they impact us all in a myriad of different ways defining lives, opportunities, and justice in a too often unjust world.

Global justice is a flourishing field. Some of the most influential names in philosophy have made important contributions to the area. This fast-growing body of work has introduced new concepts, approaches, theoretical insights, and practical innovations. These make a significant impact on both how we *understand* global justice issues and what we might *do* about them revealing horizons of possibilities for future actions.

This *Introduction* offers a survey to these topics, figures, and contributions. While a standalone book, it focuses on readings in the accompanying revised edition of *The Global Justice Reader* and intended to be read alongside it. It is hoped readers will gain a broad understanding of the main issues, challenges, and leading figures to global justice debates – so they might explore further this rich and varied field. I can reassure from my first-hand experience that this journey is enormously interesting – and its subject-matter ever-increasingly more urgent – and rewarding.

Global Justice: An Introduction, First Edition. Thom Brooks.
© 2023 John Wiley & Sons Ltd. Published 2023 by John Wiley & Sons Ltd.

Bibliography

Ackerman, Bruce (2006). *Before the Next Attack: Preserving Civil Liberties in an Age of Terrorism*. New Haven: Yale University Press.

Aquinas, St Thomas (2002). *Political Writings*. Cambridge: Cambridge University Press.

Armstrong, Chris (2012). *Global Distributive Justice: An Introduction*. Cambridge: Cambridge University Press.

Atkins, J Spencer (2018). "Have You Benefitted from Carbon Emissions? You May Be a 'Morally Objectionable Free Rider'," *Environmental Ethics* 40:283–296.

Barry, Brian (1995). "John Rawls and the Search for Stability," *Ethics* 105:874–915.

Beitz, Charles R (1999). *Political Theory and International Relations*, 2nd ed. Princeton: Princeton University Press.

Beitz, Charles R (2001). "Human Rights as a Common Concern," *American Political Science Review* 95:269–282.

Beitz, Charles R (2009). *The Idea of Human Rights*. Oxford: Oxford University Press.

Blake, Michael (2017). "On Emergencies and Emigration: How (Not) to Justify Compulsory Medical Service," *Journal of Medical Ethics* 43:566–567.

Blake, Michael (2013). "Immigration, Jurisdiction, and Exclusion," *Philosophy and Public Affairs* 41:103–130.

Brock, Gillian (2009). *Global Justice: A Cosmopolitan Account*. Oxford: Oxford University Press.

Brock, Gillian (2021). *Migration and Political Theory*. Cambridge: Polity.

Global Justice: An Introduction, First Edition. Thom Brooks.
© 2023 John Wiley & Sons Ltd. Published 2023 by John Wiley & Sons Ltd.

Bibliography

Brooks, Thom (2002a). "Cosmopolitanism and Distributing Responsibilities," *Critical Review of International Social and Political Philosophy* 5:92–97.

Brooks, Thom (2002b). "Saving the Greatest Number," *Logique et Analyse* 45:55–59.

Brooks, Thom (2007). "Punishing States That Cause Global Poverty," *William Mitchell Law Review* 33:519–532.

Brooks, Thom (ed.) (2008). *The Global Justice Reader*. Oxford: Blackwell.

Brooks, Thom (2009). "The Problem with Polygamy," *Philosophical Topics* 37:109–122.

Brooks, Thom (2010). "Justifying Terrorism," *Public Affairs Quarterly* 24:189–195.

Brooks, Thom (2011). "Rethinking Remedial Responsibilities," *Ethics and Global Politics* 4:195–202.

Brooks, Thom (ed.) (2012). *Global Justice and International Affairs*. Leiden: Brill.

Brooks, Thom (2013a). *Hegel's Political Philosophy: A Systematic Reading of the Philosophy of Right*, 2nd ed. Edinburgh: Edinburgh University Press.

Brooks, Thom (2013b). "Philosophy Unbound: The Idea of Global Philosophy," *Metaphilosophy* 44:254–266.

Brooks, Thom (ed.) (2013c). *Just War Theory*. Leiden: Brill.

Brooks, Thom (2014a). "A New Problem with the Capabilities Approach," *Harvard Review of Philosophy* 20:100–106.

Brooks, Thom (2014b). "Remedial Responsibilities Beyond Nations," *Journal of Global Ethics* 10:156–166.

Brooks, Thom (ed.) (2015a). *Current Controversies in Political Philosophy*. London: Routledge.

Brooks, Thom (2015b). "The Capabilities Approach and Political Liberalism" in Thom Brooks and Martha C Nussbaum (eds), *Rawls's Political Liberalism*. New York: Columbia University Press, pp. 139–173.

Brooks, Thom (2016a). "What is Global Justice?" in Duncan Pritchard (ed.), *What is this Thing Called Philosophy?* London: Routledge, pp. 68–80.

Brooks, Thom (2016b). *Becoming British: UK Citizenship Examined*. London: Biteback.

Brooks, Thom (2016c). "Justice as Stakeholding" in Krushil Watene and Jay Drydyk (eds), *Theorizing Justice: Critical Insights and Future Directions*. New York: Rowan and Littlefield, pp. 111–127.

Brooks, Thom (2016d). "How Not to Save the Planet," *Ethics, Policy and Environment* 19:119–132.

Brooks, Thom (2020a). *Climate Change Ethics for an Endangered World*. London: Routledge.

Brooks, Thom (ed.) (2020b). *The Oxford Handbook of Global Justice*. Oxford: Oxford University Press.

Brooks, Thom (2020c). "Capabilities, Freedom and Severe Poverty" in Thom Brooks (ed.), *The Oxford Handbook of Global Justice*. Oxford: Oxford University Press, pp. 199–213.

Brooks, Thom (2020d). "Climate Change Ethics and the Problem of End-State Solutions" in Thom Brooks (ed.), *The Oxford Handbook of Global Justice*. Oxford: Oxford University Press, pp. 241–258.

Brooks, Thom (2020e). "Collective Responsibility for Severe Poverty," *Global Policy* 11:486–491.

Brooks, Thom (2021). "Global Justice and Stakeholding," *International Journal of Applied Philosophy* 34:105–122.

Brooks, Thom (2022a). *Reforming the UK's Citizenship Test: Building Bridges, Not Barriers*. Bristol: Bristol University Press.

Brooks, Thom (2022b). *New Arrivals: A Fair Immigration Plan for Labour*. London: Fabian Society.

Brooks, Thom (2022c). *The Trust Factor: Essays on the Current Crisis and Hope for the Future*. London: Methuen.

Brooks, Thom (ed.) (2023a). *The Global Justice Reader*, revised ed. Oxford: Blackwell.

Brooks, Thom (2023b). "Cruel and Unusual Punishment" in Jesper Ryberg (ed.), *The Oxford Handbook of Punishment Theory and Philosophy*. Oxford: Oxford University Press, forthcoming.

Brooks, Thom (2024). *Political Philosophy: The Fundamentals*. Oxford: Blackwell.

Brooks, Thom and Nussbaum, Martha C (eds) (2015). *Rawls's Political Liberalism*. New York: Columbia University Press.

Brown, D Mackenzie (1953). *The White Umbrella: Indian Political Thought from Manu to Gandhi*. Westport: Greenwood Press.

Brown, Lester R (2011). *World on the Edge: How to Prevent Environmental and Economic Collapse*. New York: W. W. Norton.

Buchanan, Allen (1997). "Theories of Secession," *Philosophy and Public Affairs* 26:31–61.

Calhoun, Cheshire (2005). "Who's Afraid of Polygamous Marriage? Lessons for Same-Sex Marriage Advocacy from the History of Polygamy," *San Diego Law Review* 42:1023–1042.

Camus, Albert (1986). *Neither Victims nor Executioners*, trans. Dwight Macdonald. Philadelphia: New Society Publishers.

Caney, Simon (2001). "Cosmopolitan Justice and Equalizing Opportunities," *Metaphilosophy* 32:113–134.

Caney, Simon (2005). "Cosmopolitan Justice, Responsibility, and Global Climate Change," *Leiden Journal of International Law* 18:747–775.

Caney, Simon (2012). "Just Emissions," *Philosophy and Public Affairs* 40:255–300.

Carens, Joseph (2013). *The Ethics of Immigration*. Oxford: Oxford University Press.

Coady, Cecil Anthony John (2001). "Terrorism" in Lawrence C Becker and Charlotte B Becker (eds), *Encyclopedia of Ethics*, 2nd ed ed, Vol. 3. New York and London: Routledge, pp. 1696–1699.

Cohen, Joshua (2010). "Philosophy, Social Science, Global Poverty" in Alison M Jaggar (ed.), *Thomas Pogge and His Critics*. Cambridge: Polity, pp. 18–45.

Cole, Philip (2001). *Philosophies of Exclusion*. Edinburgh: Edinburgh University Press.

Bibliography

Convention relating to the Status of Refugees (1951). *United Nations*, url: https://www.ohchr.org/en/instruments-mechanisms/instruments/convention-relating-status-refugees.

Cruft, Rowan, Liao, S Matthew, and Renzo, Massimo (eds) (2015). *The Philosophical Foundations of Human Rights*. Oxford: Oxford University Press.

Crutzen, Paul J (2006). "Albedo Enhancement by Stratospheric Sulfur Injections: A Contribution to Resolve a Policy Dilemma?" *Climatic Change* 77:211–219.

Dill, Janina (2015). "Ending Wars: The *Jus ad Bellum* Principles Suspended, Repeated or Adjusted?" *Ethics* 125:627–630.

Dubber, Markus D (2015). *An Introduction to the Model Penal Code*, 2nd ed. Oxford: Oxford University Press.

Filmer, Robert (1991). in Johann P Sommerville (ed.), *Patriarcha and Other Writings*. Cambridge: Cambridge University Press.

Gardiner, Stephen M (2002). "The Real Tragedy of the Commons," *Philosophy and Public Affairs* 30:387–416.

Gardiner, Stephen M (2004). "Ethics and Global Climate Change," *Ethics* 114:555–600.

Gardiner, Stephen M (2011). *A Perfect Moral Storm: The Ethical Tragedy of Climate Change*. Oxford: Oxford University Press.

Garvey, James (2008). *The Ethics of Climate Change: Right and Wrong in a Warming World*. London: Continuum.

Goodin, Robert E (1988). "What Is So Special About Our Fellow Countrymen?" *Ethics* 98:663–686.

Gould, Carol C (2004). *Globalizing Democracy and Human Rights*. Cambridge: Cambridge University Press.

Green, Thomas Hill (1986). *Lectures on the Principles of Political Obligation and Other Writings*. Cambridge: Cambridge University.

Gross, Michael L (2003). "Fighting by Other Means in the Mideast: A Critical Analysis of Israel's Assassination Policy," *Political Studies* 51:350–368.

Gross, Michael L (2010). *Moral Dilemmas of Modern War: Torture, Assassination, and Blackmail in an Age of Asymmetric Conflict*. Cambridge: Cambridge University Press.

Guthrie, Charles and Quinlan, Michael (2007). *Just War: The Just War Tradition – Ethics in Modern Warfare*. London: Bloomsbury.

Hall, John A and Malesevic, Sinisa (eds) (2013). *Nationalism and War*. Cambridge: Cambridge University Press.

Hardin, Garrett (1968). "Tragedy of the Commons," *Science* 162:1243–1248.

Hardin, Garrett (1974). "Living in a Lifeboat," *Biosciences* 24:561–568.

Hart, Herbert Lionel Adolphus (2008). *Punishment and Responsibility: Essays in the Philosophy of Law*, 2nd ed. Oxford: Oxford University Press.

Hegel, Georg Wilhelm Friedrich (1991). *Elements of the Philosophy of Right*. Cambridge: Cambridge University Press.

Heider, Ulrike and Lewis, Danny (1994). *Anarchism: Left, Right and Green*. San Francisco: City Lights Books.

Held, David (2010). *Cosmopolitanism: Ideals and Realities*. Cambridge: Polity.

Held, Virginia (2008). *How Terrorism is Wrong: Morality and Political Violence*. Oxford: Oxford University Press.

Hobbes, Thomas (1996). in Richard Tuck (ed.), *Leviathan*. Cambridge: Cambridge University Press.

Hohfeld, Wesley (1919). *Fundamental Legal Conceptions as Applied in Judicial Reasoning*. New Haven: Yale University Press.

Intergovernmental Panel on Climate Change (2014). *Climate Change 2014: Impacts, Adaptation and Vulnerability*. Cambridge: Cambridge University Press.

Intergovernmental Panel on Climate Change (2019). "Special Report on the Ocean and Cryosphere in a Changing Climate: Summary for Policymakers," url: https://www.unep.org/resources/report/ipcc-special-report-ocean-and-cryosphere-changing-climate.

Intergovernmental Panel on Climate Change (2020). *Special Report: Global Warming of 1.5 °C*. Geneva: Intergovernmental Panel on Climate Change.

Jaggar, Alison M (2005). "'Saving Amina': Global Justice for Women and Intercultural Dialogue," *Ethics and International Affairs* 19:55–75.

Jaggar, Alison M (2020). "Global Gender Justice" in Thom Brooks (ed.), *The Oxford Handbook of Global Justice*. Oxford: Oxford University Press, pp. 337–361.

Jamieson, Dale (2008). *Ethics and the Environment: An Introduction*. Cambridge: Cambridge University Press.

Jenkins, Dafydd (1986). *The Law of Hywel Dda*. Llandysul: Gomer Press.

Jones, Charles and Vernon, Richard (2018). *Patriotism*. Cambridge: Polity.

Jones, Peter (1994). *Rights*. Basingstoke: Palgrave.

Jones, Peter (1999). "Group Rights and Group Oppression," *Journal of Political Philosophy* 7:353–377.

Kahn, Matthew (2010). *Climatopolis: How Our Cities Will Thrive in the Hotter Future*. New York: Basic Books.

Kant, Immanuel (1957). in Lewis White Beck (ed.), *Perpetual Peace*. Indianapolis: Bobbs-Merrill.

Kant, Immanuel (1996). *The Metaphysics of Morals*. Cambridge: Cambridge University Press.

Kleingeld, Pauline (2000). "Kantian Patriotism," *Philosophy and Public Affairs* 29:313–341.

Kleingeld, Pauline and Eric Brown (2019). "Cosmopolitanism," *Stanford Encyclopedia of Philosophy*, url: https://plato.stanford.edu/entries/cosmopolitanism/.

Lazar, Seth (2012). "Necessity in Self-Defense and War," *Philosophy and Public Affairs* 40:3–44.

Levitt, Steven D and Dubner, Stephen J (2010). *Superfreakonomics*. London: Penguin.

Locke, John (1980). *Second Treatise of Civil Government*. New York: Hackett.

Locke, John (1988). *Two Treatises of Government*. Cambridge: Cambridge University Press.

Bibliography

Lomborg, Bjørn (1998). *The Skeptical Environmentalist: Measuring the Real State of the World*. Cambridge: Cambridge University Press.

Lomborg, Bjørn (2008). *Cool It: The Skeptical Environmentalist's Guide to Global Warming*. New York: Vintage.

Lopez, George and Gordon, Neve (2000). "Terrorism in the Arab-Israeli Conflict" in Andrew Valls (ed.), *Ethics in International Affairs*. Lanham: Rowman and Littlefield, pp. 99–113.

Margalit, Avishai and Raz, Joseph (1990). "National Self-Determination," *Journal of Philosophy* 87(9):439–461.

Mason, Elinor (2001). *Feminist Philosophy: An Introduction*. London: Routledge.

Mastrandrea, Michael D and Schenider, Stephen H (2010). *Preparing for Climate Change*. Cambridge: MIT Press.

McAfee, Noelle (2018). "Feminist Philosophy," *Stanford Encyclopedia of Philosophy*, url: https://plato.stanford.edu/entries/feminist-philosophy/.

McMahan, Jeff (2005). "Just Cause for War," *Ethics and International Affairs* 19:55–75.

McMahan, Jeff (2009). *Killing in War*. Oxford: Oxford University Press.

Mill, John Stuart (1984). "A Few Words on Non-Intervention" in John M Robson (ed.), *The Collected Works of John Stuart Mill*, Vol. XXI. Toronto: University of Toronto Press, pp. 118–124.

Mill, John Stuart (1989). *On Liberty and Other Writings*. Cambridge: Cambridge University Press.

Miller, David (1976). *Social Justice*. Oxford: Oxford University Press.

Miller, David (1995). *On Nationality*. Oxford: Oxford University Press.

Miller, David (1999). *Principles of Social Justice*. Oxford: Oxford University Press.

Miller, David (2000). *Citizenship and National Identity*. Cambridge: Polity.

Miller, David (2001). "Distributing Responsibilities," *Journal of Political Philosophy* 9:453–471.

Miller, David (2007). *National Responsibility and Global Justice*. Oxford: Oxford University Press.

Miller, David (2008). "Immigrants, Nations, and Citizenship," *Journal of Political Philosophy* 16:371–390.

Miller, David (2016). *Strangers in Our Midst: The Political Philosophy of Immigration*. Cambridge: Harvard University Press.

Miller, Richard W (1998). "Cosmopolitan Respect and Patriotic Concern," *Philosophy and Public Affairs* 27:202–224.

Miller, Seumas (2017). "Torture," *Stanford Encyclopedia of Philosophy*, url: https://plato.stanford.edu/entries/torture/.

Miscevic, Nenad (2020). "Nationalism," *Stanford Encyclopedia of Philosophy*, url: https://plato.stanford.edu/entries/nationalism/.

Nagel, Thomas (1972). "War and Massacre," *Philosophy and Public Affairs* 1:123–144.

Nagel, Thomas (2003). "The Problem of Global Justice," *Philosophy and Public Affairs* 33:113–147.

Nagel, Thomas (2005). "The Problem of Global Justice," *Philosophy and Public Affairs* 33:113–147.

Nickel, James W (2007). *Making Sense of Human Rights*. Oxford: Blackwell.

Nolan, Christopher (2008). *The Dark Knight*. Burbank: Warner Brothers.

Nozick, Robert (1974). *Anarchy, State and Utopia*. New York: Basic Books.

Nussbaum, Martha C (1999). *Sex and Social Justice*. Oxford: Oxford University Press.

Nussbaum, Martha C (2000). *Women and Human Development: The Capabilities Approach*. Cambridge: Cambridge University Press.

Nussbaum, Martha C (2002). "Patriotism and Cosmopolitanism" in Joshua Cohen (ed.), *For Love of Country? Debating the Limits of Patriotism*. Boston: Beacon Press, pp. 2–17, 145.

Nussbaum, Martha C (2003). "Capabilities as Fundamental Entitlements: Sen and Social Justice," *Feminist Economics* 9:33–50.

Nussbaum, Martha C (2004). "On Hearing Women's Voices: A Reply to Susan Okin," *Philosophy and Public Affairs* 32:193–205.

Nussbaum, Martha C (2006). *Frontiers of Justice: Disability, Nationality, Species Membership*. Cambridge: Harvard University Press.

Nussbaum, Martha C (2008). *Liberty of Conscience: In Defense of America's Tradition of Religious Equality*. New York: Basic Books.

Nussbaum, Martha C (2011). *Creating Capabilities: The Human Development Approach*. Cambridge: Harvard University Press.

Okin, Susan Moller (1999). in Joshua Cohen, Matthew Howard, and Martha C Nussbaum (eds), *Is Multiculturalism Bad for Women?* Princeton: Princeton University Press.

Okin, Susan Moller (2003). "Poverty, Well-Being, and Gender: What Counts, Who's Heard?" *Philosophy and Public Affairs* 31:280–316.

O'Mara, Shane (2015). *Why Torture Doesn't Work*. Cambridge: Harvard University Press.

Parekh, Bhikhu (2006). *Rethinking Multiculturalism: Cultural Diversity and Political Theory*, 2nd ed. Basingstoke: Palgrave Macmillan.

Parekh, Bhikhu (2008). *A New Politics of Identity: Political Principles for an Interdependent World*. Basingstoke: Palgrave Macmillan.

Parekh, Bhikhu (2019). *Ethnocentric Political Theory: The Pursuit of Flawed Universals*. Basingstoke: Palgrave Macmillan.

Philpott, Daniel (2020). "Sovereignty," *Stanford Encyclopedia of Philosophy*, url: https://plato.stanford.edu/entries/sovereignty/.

Plato (1992). *Republic*, trans. G. M. A. Grube. Indianapolis: Hackett.

Plato (1997). *Complete Works*. Indianapolis: Hackett.

Pogge, Thomas W (1992). "Cosmopolitanism and Sovereignty," *Ethics* 103:48–75.

Pogge, Thomas W (2001). "Eradicating Systematic Poverty: Brief for a Global Resources Dividend," *Journal of Human Development* 2:59–77.

Pogge, Thomas W (2002). *World Poverty and Human Rights*. Cambridge: Polity.

Pogge, Thomas W (ed.) (2007). *Freedom from Poverty as a Human Right: Who Owes What to the Very Poor?* Oxford: Oxford University Press.

Bibliography

Pogge, Thomas W (2010). *Politics as Usual: What Lies Behind the Pro-Poor Rhetoric*. Cambridge: Polity.

Posner, Eric A and Weisbach, David (2010). *Climate Change Justice*. Princeton: Princeton University Press.

Primoratz, Igor (ed.) (2007). *Civilian Immunity in War*. Oxford: Oxford University Press.

Primoratz, Igor (2013). *Terrorism: A Philosophical Investigation*. Cambridge: Polity Press.

Primoratz, Igor (2022). "Terrorism," *Stanford Encyclopedia of Philosophy*, url: https://plato.stanford.edu/entries/terrorism/.

Rabin, Andrew (2020). *Crime and Punishment in Anglo-Saxon England*. Cambridge: Cambridge University Press.

Raghuramaraju, Adluru (2011). *Modernity in Indian Social Theory*. Oxford: Oxford University Press.

Rawls, John (1971). *A Theory of Justice*. Cambridge: Harvard University Press.

Rawls, John (1996). *Political Liberalism*, paperback ed. New York: Columbia University Press.

Rawls, John (1999). *The Law of Peoples*. Cambridge: Harvard University Press.

Rawls, John (2001). *Justice as Fairness: A Restatement*. Cambridge: Harvard University Press.

Risse, Mathias (2009). "The Right to Relocation: Disappearing Island Nations and Common Ownership of the Earth," *Ethics and International Affairs* 23:281–300.

Rodin, David (2004). "Terrorism without Intention," *Ethics* 114:752–771.

Royal Society (2020). "How Fast is Sea Level Rising," url: https://royalsociety.org/topics-policy/projects/climate-change-evidence-causes/question-14/.

Russett, Bruce (1993). *Grasping the Democratic Peace: Principles for a Post-Cold War World*. Princeton: Princeton University Press.

Sandel, Michael (2005). "Should We Buy the Right to Pollute?" in *Public Philosophy: Essays on Morality in Politics*. Cambridge: Harvard University Press, pp. 93–96.

Sangiovanni, Andrea (2016). "How Practices Matter," *Journal of Political Philosophy* 24:3–23.

Scharfstein, Ben-Ami (1998). *A Comparative History of Western Philosophy: From the Upanisads to Kant*. Albany: State University of New York Press.

Scheffler, Samuel (2007). "Immigration and the Significance of Culture," *Philosophy and Public Affairs* 35:93–125.

Schell, Jonathan (2020). "Nature and Value" in Akeel Bigrami (ed.), *Nature and Value*. New York: Columbia University Press, pp. 1–12.

Seglow, Jonathan (2010). "Associative Duties and Global Justice," *Journal of Moral Philosophy* 7:54–73.

Sen, Amartya (1990). "More than 100 Million Women Are Missing," *New York Review of Books* 37(December 20):61–66.

Sen, Amartya (1993). "Capability and Well-Being" in Martha C Nussbaum and Amartya Sen (eds), *The Quality of Life*. Oxford: Oxford University Press, pp. 30–53.

Sen, Amartya (1999). *Development as Freedom*. Oxford: Oxford University Press.

Sen, Amartya (2009). *The Idea of Justice*. London: Allen Lane.

Simms, Andrew (2009). *Ecological Debt: Global Warming and the Wealth of Nations*, 2nd ed. London: Pluto Press.

Singer, Peter (1972). "Famine, Affluence and Morality," *Philosophy and Public Affairs* 1:229–243.

Singer, Peter (2004). *One World: The Ethics of Globalization*, 2nd ed. New Haven: Yale University Press.

Singer, Peter (2007). *One World: The Ethics of Globalization*. New Haven: Yale University Press.

Smilansky, Saul (2004). "Terrorism, Justification, and Illusion," *Ethics* 114:790–805.

Smilansky, Saul (2007). *Ten Moral Paradoxes*. Oxford: Blackwell.

Steinhoff, Uwe (2007). *On the Ethics of War and Terrorism*. Oxford: Oxford University Press.

Stenton, Frank Merry (1971). *Anglo-Saxon England*. Oxford: Oxford University Press.

Stern, Nicholas (2009). *A Blueprint for a Safer Planet*. London: Bodley head.

Sussman, David (2005). "What's Wrong with Torture?" *Philosophy and Public Affairs* 33:1–33.

Tan, Kok-Chor (2004). *Justice Without Borders: Cosmopolitanism, Nationalism and Patriotism*. Cambridge: Cambridge University Press.

Uberoi, Varun (2018). "National Identity: A Multiculturalist's Approach," *Critical Review of International Social and Political Philosophy* 21:46–64.

United Nations (1946). *Charter*.

United Nations Environment Programme (2020). *Climate Adaptation*, url: http://www.unep.org/explore-topics/climate-change/what-we-do/climate-adaptation.

United States (1776). *Declaration of Independence*.

Universal Declaration of Human Rights (1948).

Vernon, Richard (2010). *Cosmopolitan Regard: Political Membership and Global Justice*. Cambridge: Cambridge University Press.

Wackernagel, Mathis (2009). "Methodological Advancements in Footprint Analysis," *Ecological Economics* 68:1925–1927.

Wackernagel, Mathis and Rees, William E (1996). *Our Ecological Footprint: Reducing Human Impact on the Earth*. Gabriola Island: New Society Publishers.

Waldron, Jeremy (1993). "Special Ties and Natural Duties," *Philosophy and Public Affairs* 22: 3–30.

Walzer, Michael (2000). *Just and Unjust War: A Moral Argument with Historical Illustrations*, 3rd ed. New York: Basic Books.

Walzer, Michael (2002). "Five Questions about Terrorism," *Dissent* (Winter), url: https://www.dissentmagazine.org/article/five-questions-about-terrorism.

Watene, Krushil (2020). "Transforming Global Justice Theorizing: Indigenous Philosophies" in Thom Brooks (ed.), *The Oxford Handbook of Global Justice*. Oxford: Oxford University Press, pp. 163–180.

Bibliography

Wellman, Christopher Heath (2008). "Immigration and Freedom of Association," *Ethics* 119:109–141.

Wenar, Leif (1995). "*Political Liberalism*: An Internal Critique," *Ethics* 106:32–62.

Wenar, Leif (2005). "The Nature of Rights," *Philosophy and Public Affairs* 33:223–252.

Wilkinson, Richard and Pickett, Kate (2010). *The Spirit Level: Why Equality is Better for Everyone*. Harmondsworth: Penguin.

Wisnewski, J Jeremy (2010). *Understanding Torture*. Edinburgh: Edinburgh University Press.

Wood, Allen W (2008). *Kantian Ethics*. Cambridge: Cambridge University Press.

World Bank (2018). *Nearly Half the World Lives on Less than $5.50 a Day* (17 October). New York: World Bank.

Ypi, Lea, Goodin, Robert E, and Barry, Christian (2009). "Associative Duties, Global Justice and the Colonies," *Philosophy and Public Affairs* 37:103–135.

Index

Index

Index